MILITARY INVOLVEMENT AND TRADE TREATIES

Exploring the Differences in Military Involvement of the United States in Foreign Countries, Post-Trade Treaty

THOMAS ANTHONY GUERRIERO

Order this book online at www.trafford.com
or email orders@trafford.com

Most Trafford titles are also available at major online book retailers.

Printed in the United States of America.

ISBN: 978-1-4907-2682-3 (sc)
ISBN: 978-1-4907-2683-0 (e)

Trafford rev. 01/29/2014

North America & international
toll-free: 1 888 232 4444 (USA & Canada)
fax: 812 355 4082

CONTENTS

LIST OF TABLES

LIST OF FIGURES

ABSTRACT

Every US bilateral trade treaty is a potential generator of US military involvement. The involvement of the US military in foreign states is both a domestic and international problem. This study was conducted to explore the differences in military involvement of the United States in foreign countries, post-trade treaty. This research was designed to compare bilateral trade treaties between the participating states, and explore the possible factors or conditions that differentiated the countries that showed an increase in military involvement after entering a trade treaty with the United States. This study used qualitative methodologies, utilizing a study design that focused on the examination of historical data. The findings revealed that trade treaties of the United States with foreign states that showed an increase in military involvement post-treaty reflected higher imports but lower exports compared to countries that had trade treaties with the United States that showed no increase in military involvement post-treaty. There was evidence that proximity with the United States did not play a role in the increase of military involvement post-treaty. The findings suggest that when trade is more beneficial to the bilateral trade partner of the United States, as reflected by higher import and lower export, increased military involvement of the United States could be a result. Future studies should expand the scope of the study to increase the generalizability of the results.

ACKNOWLEDGEMENTS

I would like to acknowledge and extend my heartfelt gratitude to both Professor Muhamet Bass & Professor Beth Simmons, the Director of the Weatherhead Center for International Affairs at Harvard University. They were gracious enough to make time in their busy schedules and workload to act as my strategic advisors for this book. As both my professor in International Law at Harvard and as my advisor on this book, Professor Simmons' knowledge, experience, and time were greatly appreciated throughout this journey. Without Professor Bas's effort, the creative process and the completion of this book would not have been possible. Thank you Professor Bas from the bottom of my heart for I am forever in a debt of gratitude to you.

I would like to thank Dr. Don Ostrowski for all your advice and guidance for the entire process of this book. Your knowledge and experience in this area really has contributed to my life by educating me on the art of creating, proposing, and executing the completion of my book. Your time, advice, expertise, and words of wisdom were greatly appreciated.

To my family, I want to thank my wife and my children for seeing my vision. This tremendous accomplishment would not be possible without the support of my family. Moving to Cambridge was no easy task, but you welcomed the experience because you knew how important this was to me. The long nights, the crazy travel schedules, the long summers, all of it was worth it. We did it. Thank you.

CHAPTER 1

INTRODUCTION

The involvement of the US military in foreign states is both a domestic and international problem. When the United States commits funds they do not have for military involvement in foreign states, fiscal problems could arise. Every US trade treaty is a potential generator of US military involvement on foreign soil, possibly contributing to this problem.

1.1 BACKGROUND

To enter into a bilateral trade treaty is one issue, but to commit US troops and the financial resources of the United States could be a different matter. When the United States enters into trade treaties with foreign states, there is a possibility that the installation of US military bases in foreign countries could follow.[1]

International bilateral trade treaties are generated to influence states in different sectors, which may be economic, commercial, social, or psychological in nature. The negotiation and finalization of treaty terms set parameters and expectations for the states to follow. There is growing accord that states that engage with the United States in bilateral trade treaties are active participants in the increase of the global involvement of the US military. The global community needs to be proactive in initiating constructive dialogue with their leaders to address the problem of US military involvement in foreign states, which can have a significant global influence.

The close proximity of the United States to South America suggests that proximity played a role[2] in the increase of US military involvement in recent years in this region. The number of US military bases in South America is growing faster than in any other region that is part of the US bilateral trade treaties. There seems to be an indication that the closer geographically to bilateral treaty states are in proximity, the more likely that securing US military bases in foreign states will happen. As the number of South American treaty countries with closer geographical proximity of the United States increases in number, so does the issue of US military strategy in the region. Despite these suggestions, there is no empirical evidence indicating that proximity of foreign countries to the United States plays a role in the increase of military involvement.

Although there are established guidelines for gaining approval to commit financial and military resources, there is a need for clear legislation and a national policy on US military

---

[1]   "Thailand: Background and US Relations," last modified June 5, 2012. http://www.fas.org/sgp/crs/row/RL32593.pdf.

[2]   "Pentagon Building Bases in Central America and Colombia," last modified January 27, 2011.http://forusa.org/blogs/john-linsay-poland/pentagon-building-bases-central-america-colombia/8445.

involvement in foreign states. This study sought to explore the participation of the United States in trade treaties and the effect of trade treaties in US military involvement in foreign states. The history of the United States regarding bilateral trade treaties was examined to gain insights on the topic of this study.

1.2 AREA OF STUDY

A trade treaty may bring opportunities, improve access to information, introduce technology, introduce products, and introduce a multitude of services.[3] Critics who oppose trade treaties argued that these opportunities have come at the expense of poorer, less developed countries, clearing the way for the more dominant country to benefit significantly more from these treaties. Hagan argued that the United States tends to benefit more from these bilateral treaties than the other participating countries.[4]

The United States has a vast network of trade partners throughout the world,[5] with over a thousand military bases around the world.[6] Trade treaties are intended to increase the supply of goods, provide lower prices, and increase product selection between the United States and the participating states.[7] These bilateral trade treaties could also serve as the impetus for securing diplomatic or political advantages for the participating states, such as military or financial aid.[8]

The role of bilateral trade treaties in securing of US military bases in foreign countries is not clear. However, the United States' relations with other countries, such as through treaties and financial aid, is rooted in the premise that the United States expects to gain advantages and benefits from these relations. Benefits that the United States could gain from these relations may be economic, political, or diplomatic in nature.[9]

The proximity between the United States and the partner state in the bilateral trade treaties suggests that geographical proximity could have a role in increasing US military involvement in foreign states.[10] Nations in close geographical proximity share common interests, which suggests that there may be common elements in culture, religion, language, history, social, and economic systems among such nations. However, no empirical evidence exists that supports this suggestion. This thesis involved a comparative analysis between states that entered into bilateral

---

[3]   "Taking Advantage of Free Trade Agreements in Order to Export," last modified January 30, 2008. http://voices.yahoo.com/taking-advantage-free-trade-agreements-order-845137.html.

[4]   "Taking Advantage of Free Trade Agreements."

[5]   "The Worldwide Network of US Military Bases: The Global Deployment of US Military Personnel," last modified February 17, 2013.http://www.globalresearch.ca/the-worldwide-network-of-us-military-bases/5564.

[6]   Hugh Gusterson, *People of the Bomb: Portraits of America's Nuclear Complex* (Minneapolis: University of Minnesota Press, 2004).

[7]   "US-Latin American Trade: Recent Trends and Policy Issues," last modified February 8, 2011.http://www.fas.org/sgp/crs/row/98-840.pdf.

[8]   "US-UK Relations at the Start of the 21st Century," last modified January 2006.http://www.strategicstudiesinstitute.army.mil/pdffiles/pub633.pdf.

[9]   "US-UK Relations."

[10] "Israel: Background and U.S. Relations," last modified November 7, 2012. http://www.fas.org/sgp/crs/mideast/RL33476.pdf.

trade treaties with the United States around the world, compared to participating states in the South America region (Chile, Peru, Colombia), a region geographically closest to the United States. The effect of the involvement of the US military in the states where bilateral partnerships exist was examined by measuring the US military's involvement in that state both pre-treaty and post-treaty.[11]

This research, conducted at Harvard University, was designed to contribute to the existing body of research concerning the possible factors that contribute to the increase of US military involvement around the world. The motivation was to make a significant contribution to the existing body of research by comparing the influence of US bilateral treaty states around the world. This study will provide insights that might allow for a more effective international policy for the United States concerning trade treaties and military involvement in foreign states.

1.3 RESEARCH OBJECTIVES

This section contains the research objectives of the study. The section is organized into two sub-sections: general objective and specific objectives. Each of the sub-sections will be discussed next.

1.3.1 GENERAL OBJECTIVES

The main objectives of this study were to explore the increase in US military involvement post-treaty as it relates to bilateral trade treaties, and to examine the significance of proximity concerning these US bilateral trade treaties. Through these objectives, the historic bilateral treaties were examined, including the effect of bilateral treaties in terms of military involvement. The results of the study may be significant in the future of US foreign policy in bilateral treaties.

1.3.2 SPECIFIC OBJECTIVES

The specific objectives of this study were the following:
1. To compare the countries that showed an increase in military involvement after entering a trade treaty with the United States to countries that did not show an increase in military involvement after entering a trade treaty with the United States
2. To explore the factors and conditions differentiating countries that showed an increase in military involvement after entering a trade treaty with the United States
3. To determine if proximity to the United States is a significant factor in terms of increased military presence.

---

[11] "US Military: Mission: Possible," last modified December 1, 2010. http://latintrade.com/2010/12/u-s-military-mission-possible.

1.4 METHODOLOGY IN BRIEF

This study involved the use of a qualitative methodology, drawing on a historical review for the study design as explained by Plummer, Cheong, and Hamanaka[12] in their assessment on the influence of free trade agreements. Their study involved a qualitative evaluation of the trade effects of Free Trade Agreement's (FTA) and a comparison of trade and production levels before and after the implementation of Free Trade Agreements, using the following criteria: an increase in imports from US bilateral trade treaty partner's states accompanied by a drop in domestic production indicates an increase in trade between the two engaged states, and an increase in imports from US bilateral trade treaty partners accompanied by a drop in imports from these partners indicates a trade diversion.

This study was based on the methodology used by Plummer, Cheong, and Hamanaka. This was implemented by examining the changes in the US military involvement in the foreign state from pre-treaty to post-treaty. This was examined by identifying the number of military bases in the foreign state before and after the US bilateral treaty. This comparison provided information needed to answer the research questions.

All seventeen US bilateral trade treaties were examined, wherein two main groups were established. Group one was comprised of eleven states (Costa Rica, Guatemala, Jordan, Dominican Republic, El Salvador, Honduras, Nicaragua, South Korea, Singapore, Oman, and Morocco). This group showed no changes in US military involvement post-treaty. Group one was further divided into two sub-groups. Group one-A included states that had zero military involvement pre-treaty and post-treaty. This sub-group included Costa Rica, Guatemala, and Jordan. Group one-B included states that already had military involvement pre-treaty, but the extent of military involvement did not change post-treaty. This sub-group included Dominican Republic, El Salvador, Honduras, Korea, Morocco, Nicaragua, Oman, and Singapore. Group two was comprised of five states (Australia, Bahrain, Chile, Israel, and Peru). These states showed an increase in US military involvement post-treaty. Colombia was excluded from the group even though there was an increase in military involvement post-treaty because the United States already had military presence in Colombia pre-treaty. The qualitative data were examined and presented based on the theoretical framework.

1.4.1 RESEARCH QUESTIONS

The research questions of the study were:
1. Is there a difference between countries that showed an increase in military involvement after entering a trade treaty with the United States compared to countries that did not show an increase in military involvement after entering a trade treaty with the United States?
2. Is there a difference in US military involvement when comparing foreign states close in proximity to the United States to foreign states not close in proximity to the United States?

---

[12] "Methodology for Impact Assessment of Free Trade Agreements," last modified 2011.http://www.iadb.org/intal/intalcdi/PE/2011/07645.pdf.

3. What factors/conditions differentiate countries that showed an increase in military involvement after entering a trade treaty with the United States?

1.5 THESIS OUTLINE

Chapter one provided the introduction of the study. Chapter two contains a review of related literature as well as background literature to provide fundamental themes reflected from the research questions. At the end of the chapter, the theoretical framework explains the structure of the data analysis used in this study. Chapter three further explains the qualitative findings that were mentioned previously. Chapter four presents the empirical findings in relation to the theoretical framework discussed in Chapter two. Chapter five provides the conclusions and recommendations drawn from the discussion of the finding.

CHAPTER 2

LITERATURE AND THEORETICAL FRAMEWORK

This chapter contains the literature review and the theoretical framework used in the analysis of the findings. Some key concepts and terminologies that are relevant to this thesis are introduced, followed by an analysis of the relevant literature. This detailed review of the literature has several sub-sections. The first sub-section contains a general review of the historical accounts of US trade treaties. In the second sub-section, the research reviews the literature on the seventeen US bilateral trade treaties currently in effect with foreign states. The succeeding sub-sections contain discussions and literature comparing and contrasting the similarities and differences among the different states that are part of bilateral trade treaties with the United States. In the last sub-section, the study presents the research on proximity and the significance of proximity in military involvement.

2.1 KEY CONCEPTS AND TERMINOLOGIES

In this section, a number of concepts and terminologies are explained. These include US bilateral trade treaties, military involvement, military bases, military troops, and an overview of the relationship between trade treaties and military involvement.

2.1.1 US BILATERAL TRADE TREATIES

The United States has entered into seventeen trade treaties with foreign states.[13] These states include: Australia, Bahrain, Chile, Colombia, Costa Rica, Dominican Republic, El Salvador, Guatemala, Honduras, Israel, Jordan, Morocco, Nicaragua, Oman, Peru, Singapore, and South Korea.[14]

2.1.2 US MILITARY INVOLVEMENT

In this study, military involvement was defined primarily as the establishment of new US military bases and troops in foreign states after the establishment of bilateral trade treaty.

---

[13] "Office of the United States Trade Representative," last modified 2013. http://www.ustr.gov/trade-agreements.

[14] "Office of the United States Trade Representative."

Information regarding military involvement was difficult to gather because of the secrecy involved to protect national interests.

2.1.3 US MILITARY BASES

United States military bases in foreign states were chosen as the primary factor in determining US military involvement because of the availability of data containing the number of bases installed in foreign countries. There are over 1,000 US bases that are established around the world.[15] Using military bases remains a military strategy intended to protect the interest of the country.[16]

2.1.4 US MILITARY TROOPS

For this study, US military troops on the ground in foreign states were chosen as a secondary factor that shows a relationship between US bilateral trade treaties and US military involvement. Information is available regarding the number of US troops around the world, but the information is not as concrete as the available research on military bases. For this reason, information on US military troops was only used as a complementary factor to measure military involvement.

2.1.5 RELATIONSHIP BETWEEN TRADE TREATIES AND MILITARY INVOLVEMENT

The central theoretical goal of trade treaties has been to reduce trade restrictions, allowing for a free flow of trade between the participating countries.[17] For most of the nineteenth century, and the beginning of the twentieth century, protectionist interest influenced US trade policies.[18] This perspective changed with the passing of the Reciprocal Trade Agreements Act (RTAA) in 1934.[19] The legislation amended the 1930 Smoot-Hawley Tariff Act to allow the President to negotiate reciprocal trade agreements with foreign governments. During the years before World War I, the United States confronted a variety of threats that could only be overcome through either diplomacy or military action of the state.[20]

---

[15] "How US Taxpayers Are Paying the Pentagon to Occupy the Planet," last modified December 14, 2012.http://www.aljazeera.com/indepth/opinion/2012/12/20121213122226666895.html.

[16] "Assessing US FTA Policy," last modified November 2004.http://www.petersoninstitute.org/publications/chapters_preview/375/13iie3616.pdf.

[17] "Free Trade Agreements: Impact on US Trade and Implications for US Trade Policy," last modified June 18, 2012.http://www.fas.org/sgp/crs/row/RL31356.pdf.

[18] "Free Trade Agreements: Impact."

[19] "From Smoot-Hawley to Reciprocal Trade Agreement: Changing the Course of US Trade Policy in the 1930s," last modified January 1998. http://www.nber.org/chapters/c6899.pdf.

[20] "Protectionist Empire: Trade, Tariffs, and United States Foreign Policy, 1890-1914," last modified 2011. http://government.arts.cornell.edu/assets/psac/sp11/Fordham_PSAC_Mar11.pdf.

The Reciprocal Trade Agreements Act (RTAA) enabled the United States to expand global reach through international trade. Policy makers during 1890-1914 built up American military power and sought a larger political role for the United States in world politics.[21] As a result, the country's military and diplomatic bureaucracy expanded to accommodate foreign policy activism.[22] In recent years, the United States has established or proposed negotiations to implement bilateral free trade arrangements with a number of trading states.[23]

These free trade arrangements are not new with the U.S. trade policy. Trade is critical to America's prosperity, because it fuels economic growth, supports employment, raises living standards, and increase affordable goods and services. The United States has established free trade agreements with Israel that dates back to 1985 and with Canada since 1989.[24] Vicenza, Italy, has also been home to another major US base, Camp Ederle, since 1955.[25] These bases are among the more than 1,000 bases the United States have worldwide.[26]

2.2 REVIEW OF RELATED LITERATURE

This section contains four segments. The first sub-section contains a review of the historical account of treaties involving the United States. The second sub-section contains the overview of Group one and Group two states. The third sub-section involves the discussion of the increase in US military involvement post-treaty in Group two states.

The fourth sub-section contains discussions on the significance of proximity on military involvement.

2.2.1 HISTORICAL ACCOUNT OF TREATIES INVOLVING THE UNITED STATES

In the past, the United States has used trade treaties to pursue interests that range from economic, diplomatic, military, and political benefits.[27] As the epicenter of world trade, the United States uses trade leverage to impose military involvement in countries with which it has bilateral trade treaties. This section involves a historical account intended to document how the United States has used trade agreements to pursue national interests, such as increasing military involvement in foreign states.

1700-1799. On June 1, 1776, the Continental Congress created the "Model Treaty" to help guide foreign relations and trade.[28] The Model Treaty served as a template for commercial treaties that the United States Congress sought to make with France and Spain, in order to

---

21 "Protectionist Empire."
22 "Protectionist Empire."
23 "Free Trade Agreements: Impact."
24 "Free Trade Agreements: Impact."
25 "How US Taxpayers are Paying the Pentagon."
26 "How US Taxpayers are Paying the Pentagon."
27 "US-UK Relations."
28 "Diplomatic History of the American Revolution," last modified 1985. http://www.loc.gov/rr/ program/bib/ourdocs/alliance.html.

secure military assistance in the struggle against the British in the American Revolution.[29] On September 24, 1776, Congress accepted the Model Treaty, resulting in the signing of the Treaty of Military Alliance, also known as the Treaty of Alliance.[30]

Under the leadership of Commander-in-Chief General George Washington, the United States began to recruit officers and create organizational structures to develop the Continental Army with the help of the parameters of the Treaty of Alliance.[31] The Treaty of Alliance established the relationship between the United States and France, which helped initialize the Continental Army to combat Britain.[32] This treaty became the marking point of the independence of the United States from Britain, and the beginning of US military involvement in treaty states.

In October of 1782, the Continental Congress developed a Treaty of Amity and Commerce between the United States and the Dutch Republic.[33] The United States formed an alliance with the Dutch Republic, making the Dutch Republic the second European country to recognize the Continental Congress.[34] After the Treaty of Alliance was ratified, Dutch bankers financed US military expansion and war supplies with a loan of two million dollars.[35]

The United States and Sweden signed the Treaty of Amity and Commerce on April 3, 1783. This treaty was introduced and executed by Benjamin Franklin and His Majesty King Gustav III of Sweden.[36] After the treaty was established, an increase in US military involvement in Sweden occurred. This US military strategy resulted in many Swedes fighting in the American Civil War for the Union Army, which contributed to their ultimate military success.[37] During the Cold War, the Swedish government received military aid from the United States.[38]

1800-1899. The first formal treaty between the United States and the Kingdom of Siam (Thailand) was signed during the reign of King Rama III and the Presidency of Andrew Jackson in 1833.[39] After the treaty, the United States sustained military-to-military cooperation with Siam, making the country an important element of US strategic presence in the Asian Pacific.[40] After the trade treaty, military relations between the United States and the Asia-Pacific region were established.

---

[29] "Diplomatic History."

[30] "A Brief Profile of the Continental Army," last modified 2008. http://revwar75.com/ob/intro.htm.

[31] "Trading for Security: Military Alliances and Economic Agreements," last modified 2001.http://atop. rice.edu/download/publications/LongLeedsJPR.pdf.

[32] "A Brief Profile."

[33] Jonathan Israel, *The Dutch Republic: Its Rise, Greatness, and Fall 1477-1806* (Oxford: Oxford University Press, 1995).

[34] Israel, *The Dutch Republic.*

[35] Israel, *The Dutch Republic.*

[36] "Relationship between US and Swedish Militaries.US-Sweden Defense Industry Conference," last modified June 10, 2009.http://www.ndia.org/Divisions/Divisions/International/Documents/ Michael%20Moore%20-%20Relationship%20between%20U.S.%20and%20Swedish%20militaries. pdf.

[37] "Relationship between US and Swedish Militaries."

[38] "Relationship between US and Swedish Militaries."

[39] "Looking Back: A Brief History of Thai-US Relations," last modified July 4, 2012.http://www. phuketgazette.net/phuketlifestyle/savepdf.php?ref=20127531133&id=16337.

[40] "Thailand: Background."

Cobra Gold, which is the largest US training exercise in the Asia-Pacific, was established after the US-Thailand Treaty.[41] This annual multinational training held in Thailand involved more than twenty participating countries, which was critical in improving coordination among different operations in different countries.[42] After the US-Thailand treaty, US military involvement was established in Thailand by allowing US Air Force units to use Thai air bases.[43]

The Treaty of Wang Hiya is a diplomatic agreement between the United States and China, which was signed on July 3, 1844, in the Kun Iam Temple.[44] The official name of the treaty was the Treaty of Peace, Amity, and Commerce between the United States of America and the Chinese Empire.[45] Following passage by the US Congress, President John Tyler ratified the treaty on January 17, 1845. Since the ratification of the treaty, the United States has maintained a military presence in China. Through the 1850s, the United States established the East Indies Squadron, which actively supported the defense of Republic of China on Taiwan against the Communist-led People's Republic of China (PRC). As the US-China Treaty evolved, the US military became more involved with US military forces such as the US Army, Marines, and later, the US Air Force, playing a major part in the military history of China.

1900-1984. On November 18, 1901, the United States and the United Kingdom signed the Hay-Pauncefote Treaty.[46] After the treaty was ratified, US Air Force bases in five cities in the United Kingdom were established.[47] After the treaty, US Strategic Air Forces in Europe (USAFE) also expanded.

2.2.2 OVERVIEW OF GROUP ONE AND GROUP TWO STATES (1985-PRESENT)

This sub-section contains a brief overview of the two groups of states that have bilateral trade treaties with the United States. The presentation is divided into two groups. The first group includes Costa Rica, Dominican Republic, El Salvador, Guatemala, Honduras, Jordan, Morocco, Nicaragua, Oman, Singapore, and South Korea. All of these states showed no difference in US military involvement, post-treaty. The second group includes Australia, Bahrain, Chile, Israel, and Peru. All of these states showed an increase in US military involvement, post-treaty.

Group one. Several factors have facilitated an increase in US military involvement in states that have bilateral trade treaties with the United States. The United States has seventeen established bilateral treaties with foreign states. Of those seventeen trade treaties, eleven states showed no difference in US military involvement post-treaty. These states include: Costa Rica, Dominican Republic, El Salvador, Guatemala, Honduras, Jordan, Morocco, Nicaragua, Oman, Singapore, and South Korea. For this study, these states are referred to as Group one. The treaties in the eleven states comprising Group one were similar in that they have higher rankings in the import and export of goods, compared to Group two states. The bilateral treaties

---

[41] "Cobra Gold Begins in Thailand," last modified February 8, 2012. http://www.army.mil/article/73324/.

[42] "Cobra Gold."

[43] "Looking Back: A Brief History."

[44] "China-US Trade Issues," last modified May 21, 2012. http://www.fas.org/sgp/crs/row/RL33536.pdf.

[45] "China-US Trade Issues."

[46] "US-UK Relations."

[47] "US-UK Relations."

were structured to increase the economic benefit between the states by increasing imports and exports. Despite the bilateral treaties, US military involvement in these foreign treaty states did not increase.

Group two. The six remaining bilateral trade states were states that showed an increase in US military involvement, post-treaty. These states include Australia, Bahrain, Chile, Colombia, Israel, and Peru. These bilateral states are referred to as Group two in the study. Similarities between the treaty states in Group two helped to identify the factors that might have influenced the increase in US military involvement post-treaty. The similarity among the Group two states was that the US trade ranking with Group two states was not as highly ranked as with the group of eleven treaty states in Group one. Group two states have low ranking when it comes to imports and exports.

2.2.3 INCREASE IN US MILITARY INVOLVEMENT POST-TREATY IN GROUP TWO STATES

This sub-section reviews Group two states (Australia, Bahrain, Chile, Israel, and Peru) and Colombia. The review was generated from the seventeen bilateral trade treaties entered in by the United States with foreign states. The purpose of this presentation is to provide information regarding the pre-treaty and post-treaty US military involvement in each of these foreign states to show the possible reasons why Group two showed an increase in US military involvement, while Group one did not.

US-Israel treaty. The United States-Israel Free Trade Agreement was established in 1985.[48] The US House of Representatives ratified the Trade Agreement on May 7, 1985, successfully passing the US Senate on May 23, 1985.[49] The treaty was responsible for removing trade barriers between the two countries, strengthening historic friendship, and promoting transparency in trade regulations. Post-treaty, the US Navy established the United States Sixth Fleet Military Base in the Port of Haifa.[50] In 2008, both the Dimona Radar Facility and the American-operated radar base in Negev were established. These bases were staffed with 120 full-time US military personnel.[51]

US-Australia treaty. The US-Australia Free Trade Agreement was ratified by the United States on January 1, 2005.[52] After the treaty was ratified, US military involvement in Australia increased. On November 14, 2011, The US Marine Corps established Robertson Barracks, a US Marine military base in the northern part of Australia.[53] The US military became more involved,

---

[48]   "Israel: Background."

[49]   "Israel: Background."

[50]   "Port of Haifa Study: Summary Report," last modified May 1993.http://www.cna.org/sites/default/files/research/2793008910.pdf.

[51]   "How a US Radar Station in the Negev Affect a Potential Israel-Iran Clash," last modified May 30, 2012.http://www.time.com/time/world/article/0,8599,2115955,00.html.

[52]   "Free Trade Agreement: Case of US-Australia Free Trade Agreement (AUSFTA)," last modified May 2004.http://faculty.arts.ubc.ca/nmalhotra/Misc/AUSFTA-HOM-Model.pdf.

[53]   "The Marine Corps Heads Down Under: US to set up base in Australia to ward off growing China threat," last modified November 14, 2011. http://www.dailymail.co.uk/news/article-2060412/U-S-Marines-set-base-Australia-bid-beat-threat-China--sparking-fears-terror-target.html.

expanding the number of US Marines from 500 to 1000 after China's global military threat to Australia.[54]

US-Bahrain treaty. On September 14, 2004, US Trade Representative Robert B. Zoellick signed a Free Trade Agreement between United States and Bahrain. Under US and Bahrain treaty relations, the Naval Support Activity in Bahrain was established.[55] This is a United States Navy base, situated in the Kingdom of Bahrain, and is home to US Naval Forces Central Command and United States Fifth Fleet.[56] The base was developed to support Operation Enduring Freedom (OEF), and serves as the primary base in the region for naval and marine activities.[57] In March 2009, the United States Air Force established a camp on Isa Air Base to support aerial port operations.[58]

US-Chile treaty. The United States-Chile Free Trade Agreement entered into force on January 1, 2004. On July 31, 2005, an agreement was established regarding the exchange of military personnel between the United States and Chile. This agreement was established following the United States-Chile Free Trade Agreement of 2004. The goal of the trade agreement was to instill stronger discipline than WTO agreements and enforce international laws and trades. The US House of Representatives and Senate passed the trade agreement in July 2003. The United States and Chile concluded the comprehensive bilateral free trade agreement on December 11, 2012.

US-Peru treaty. The United States and Peru signed the United States-Peru Trade Promotion Agreement (PTPA) on April 12, 2006. The Peruvian Congress ratified the Agreement on June 28, 2006, and endorsed a Protocol of Amendment in June 2007. The US House of Representatives ratified the agreement on November 2, 2007, and it was approved by the US Senate on December 4, 2007. On December 14, 2007, the United States-Peru Trade Promotion Agreement Implementation Act became law, and the PTPA entered into force on February 1, 2009.

US-Colombia treaty. Colombia signed the United States-Colombia Trade Promotion Agreement (CTPA) trade treaty with the United States on November 22, 2006. The US Congress then took on the agreement, passing the agreement on October 12, 2011. The agreement went into effect on May 15, 2012.

2.2.4 SIGNIFICANCE OF PROXIMITY

This sub-section details the relevant literature on the significance of proximity when evaluating US bilateral trade treaties. All US bilateral treaty states in Group two have shown an increase in US military involvement post-treaty. Even though there is no empirical evidence that supports the role of geographical proximity in increasing military involvement of the United States after a trade treaty, the literature suggests that proximity can be a critical factor in determining the extent of US military involvement in foreign treaty states.

---

[54]   "The Marine Corps Heads Down Under."
[55]   "Bahrain: Reform, Security, and US Policy," last modified February 12, 2013.http://www.fas.org/sgp/crs/mideast/95-1013.pdf.
[56]   "Bahrain: Reform."
[57]   "Bahrain: Reform."
[58]   "Bahrain: Reform."

States form trade agreements with the United States for a number of economic[59] and political reasons.[60] The closer in proximity a state is to the United States, the more likely that their trade relationship will influence the United States on either level.[61] Most bilateral trade treaties eliminate tariffs and some non-tariff barriers. These trade agreements permit products between both states, giving easier access to each other's markets, especially with states closer in proximity to each other.[62] Proximity plays a major role in the increase of trade post-treaty. For example, in the seven years since the US-Chile Free Trade Agreement went into effect, US exports to Chile increased by 300 percent, growing from $2.7 billion in 2003 to $10.9 billion in 2010.[63]

The US-Colombia bilateral trade treaty influenced the overall trade in goods, growing from $16 billion in 2006 to $18 billion in 2007, which was critical to US national security in working with Colombia to fight against the Colombian drug cartels. Post-treaty, the US trade with Colombia increased by 12.5%. Exports of the United States to Peru grew 37% in 2010.

A bilateral trade treaty may be an easy substitute for a difficult multilateral arrangement. Often, nations in close geographical proximity share common interests. There may be common elements in culture, religion, language, history, social, and economic systems among such nations. An example of this is Indonesia's size and strategic proximity to Australia. The two countries have continued to maintain mutual diplomatic relations, formal cooperation, and broadening treaty relationships. In recent years, Australia has continued to be a committed aid to Indonesia.

Proximity has also played a significant role in the increase of US military involvement in states that are part of US bilateral trade treaties. An example can be found in Singapore's long-standing military relations with the United States. The United States sells arms to Singapore and provides access to its bases to train Singapore's armed services outside of their small city-state. Under the US-Singapore Strategic Framework Agreement, some US Navy combat ships are based in Singapore.[64] Proximity between the two states could be one of the factors that allowed for the exchange of military arms, bases, and training. More specifically, the United States and Singapore enjoy a close security relationship. Bilateral defense cooperation has deepened since the signing of the Strategic Framework Agreement in 2005, and both militaries interact regularly through joint exercises, operations, training, and technological collaboration. Starting in 2013, Singapore will host the first of four United States Combat Ships on a rotational basis.[65]

The relationship between the United States and Latin America has brought forth a post trade-treaty US military presence, which can be attributed to the proximity between the United States and Latin American states among other several factors. In 2009, the United States made an agreement with Colombia to expand military personnel in seven bases, from 250 to 800 American troops with 600 civilian contractors, effectively taking control over these installations.

---

[59] "Free Trade Agreements: Impact."

[60] "Assessing US FTA Policy."

[61] Nico Meyer, *Bilateral and Regional Trade Agreements and Technical Barriers to Trade: An African Perspective* (Johannesburg: Juta, 2010).

[62] "Trade Agreements: Impact on US Trade and Implications for US Trade Policy," last modified July 10, 2007. http://fpc.state.gov/documents/organization/89919.pdf.

[63] Meyer, *Bilateral and Regional Trade Agreements.*

[64] "Thailand: Background."

[65] "Thailand: Background."

In Honduras, which is also geographically near to the United States, US military presence was also experienced in Honduras from 2009 to 2010. Part of the motivation of the United States was to maintain control of Soto Cano's Air base through the 550 US troops and 650 US and Honduran civilians.[66]

2.3 STUDY AREA

In this section, the focus is on providing information that can explain the research problem. The proximity of all seventeen bilateral treaty states to the United States will be discussed. In this section, the discussion will be organized into two main sub-sections. The first sub-section involves the general discussion of proximity of Group one and two states to the United States. The second sub-section involves the discussion of the threats to US national security because of proximity.

2.3.1 PROXIMITY OF BILATERAL TRADE STATES WITH THE UNITED STATES

Proximity is defined as the geographic nearness of two spaces with each other. The bilateral trade relations between Group one and two states and the United States are of significant interest to American policymakers. It is of national interest and security for the United States to have prosperous and democratic bilateral trade relations with other countries. Below shows the geographical proximity in miles of the states from Group one and two to the United States.

Group One States:

US-Guatemala: Distance between the two states (1511.64 miles)
US-Honduras: Distance between the two states (1622.06 miles)
US-El Salvador: Distance between the two states (1665.42 miles)
US-Nicaragua: Distance between the two states (1797.42 miles)
US-Dominican Republic: Distance between the two states (2000.78 miles)
US-Costa Rica: Distance between the two states (2033.55 miles)
US-Morocco: Distance between the two states (4875.54 miles)
US-South Korea: Distance between the two states (6682.65 miles)
US-Jordan: Distance between the two states (6830.95 miles)
US-Oman: Distance between the two states (7995.21 miles)
US-Singapore: Distance between the two states (9511.35 miles)

Group Two States:

US-Colombia: Distance between the two states (2626.56 miles)
US-Peru: Distance between the two states (3471.34 miles)
US-Chile: Distance between the two states (5266.95 miles)

---

[66]   "Washington behind the Honduras coup: Here is the evidence," last modified July 15, 2009. http://www.globalresearch.ca/washington-behind-the-honduras-coup-here-is-the-evidence/14390.

US-Israel: Distance between the two states (6755.68 miles)
US-Bahrain: Distance between the two states (7562.11 miles)
US-Australia: Distance between the two states (9445.77 miles)

Among the Group one states, Singapore was the farthest from the United States (9511.35 miles), whereas Guatemala was the nearest (1511.64 miles) Among the six states in Group two, Australia was the farthest from the United States (9445.77 miles), whereas Colombia was the nearest (2626.56 miles).

2.3.2 THREATS TO US NATIONAL SECURITY DUE TO PROXIMITY

Many threats to US national security exist based on proximity of other nations to the US. These threats may include terrorism, espionage, and transnational criminal groups, to name a few. These threats will be discussed in the subsequent section.

Terrorism. Terrorist attacks within the Western Hemisphere in 2010 were committed primarily by two foreign terrorist organizations: the Revolutionary Armed Forces of Colombia, and the National Liberation Army, both of which are radical leftist Andean groups. After the terrorist attacks in Colombia, the United States developed the National Strategy for Combating Terrorism. With the ability of the United States to build trade agreements, the fight against terrorist organizations reached at the global level. The United States made the commitment of eradicating terrorism at the root level.

Espionage. El Salvador is one of the geographically closest states that have bilateral trade relations with the United States. The proximity between the two has come to a disadvantage to the United States with regard to espionage. For example, in 2001, Ana Delen Montes, a former senior analyst at the Defense Intelligence Agency (DIA) in the United States admitted to telling Cuban intelligence officers about a clandestine US Army camp in El Salvador. The allegation was that Montes knew about the existence of the Special Forces camp because she visited the camp a few weeks before the attack in 1987.

Transnational criminal groups. In terms of transnational criminal groups, the proximity between the United States and Colombia can pose a grave danger to the United States. Transnational terrorists and criminals may collaborate, share tactics, and benefit from interaction, resulting in bolstered capabilities, enhanced organizational infrastructure, improved access to resources, and expanded geographic reach. Historical examples also indicate that transnational criminal groups may evolve, converge, transform, or alter their ideological motivations and organizational composition to appear similar. An example of transnational criminal groups is the United Self Defense Forces of Colombia, an organization that encouraged drug trafficking worldwide.

2.3.3 THREE CASES INVOLVING PROXIMITY AND US MILITARY INVOLVEMENT

In 1940, the United States and Colombia established a bilateral agreement. Shortly after the agreement, the United States provided US military training missions and strengthened pre-World

War II relations between Bogota and Washington.[67] As relations between the two states became stronger, Colombia's position as a close ally of the United States became evident during World War II. While overextending during World War II assisting Colombia, the United States felt the effects of exposure. Colombia turned away from the support of the United States, by ordering the US troops out of Colombia.

Proximity between the United States and Nicaragua has been both beneficial and detrimental to their relations. Around the 1910s, the United States deployed US Marines to Nicaragua with the purpose of protecting American investments in the area. This maintained a general calm in the larger Panama Canal, and the United States was committed to keeping other nations from causing barriers to the transoceanic canal. The intent of the US Military to protect against barriers was soon detected. Under the command of General Augusto C. Sandino, US Marines were withdrawn in 1933.

The third event wherein proximity exposed the United States occurred with the Dominican Republic. The interest of the United States in the Dominican Republic was based on the country's democratic, stable, and economically healthy state.[68] The Dominican Republic stands as the largest Caribbean economy, the second largest country in terms of population, second largest country in terms of landmass, and an important partner in hemispheric affairs. The proximity between the United States and the Dominican Republic was one of the factors that allowed US military to easily transition to and from both states.

In April 1963, the US aircraft USS Boxer evacuated one thousand American civilians due to a riot in Dominican Republic.[69] The riot led President Johnson to order US Marines deployed to Santo Domingo to retaliate. The proximity between the United States and the Dominican Republic was what facilitated the aircrafts to be flown back and forth after Dominican rebels infiltrated the United States. This type of relationship between states was one of the bases for the United States to engage in clear bilateral trade treaties. The clear expectations of these treaties protect the United States from a change in foreign policy or political movement.

---

[67] "US Bases in Colombia Rattle the Region," last modified March 2010. http://progressive.org/danglmarch10.html.

[68] "A Fresh Look at Soft Law," last modified 1999. http://www.ejil.org/pdfs/10/3/597.pdf.

[69] "A Fresh Look at Soft Law."

CHAPTER 3

METHODOLOGY

In this chapter, I present the methodology adopted for this study. The chapter includes discussions on the qualitative research approach, the research collection methods, sampling procedure, the processing of information, and data analysis methods.

3.1 QUALITATIVE APPROACH

This study utilized qualitative methodologies to attain the goals of this research. The objective of this study was to examine how US trade treaties with foreign states increase US military involvement in those countries. The role of proximity in bilateral trade treaties as a significant factor in the extent of the US military involvement was also explored. The research questions were answered using qualitative data, which involved the thorough examination of US military involvement post-treaty and the role of proximity in US military involvement.

In this study, US trade treaties, US military involvement, and proximity were examined. Evaluating statistical data alone would not provide clarity concerning the different ways to examine the research topics of this study. Qualitative research was appropriate, because the method allowed for a deeper understanding of the existing literature. The area of interest was to explore the available literature regarding the role of proximity in US military involvement in bilateral trade treaties.

3.2 RESEARCH DESIGN

The qualitative study was designed to explore US bilateral trade treaties and US military involvement after these treaties were established. The first step was to establish a historical timeline of US bilateral treaties. The seventeen states that were involved in bilateral trade treaties with the United States were divided into two groups. States that did not show an increase in US military involvement post-treaty were named Group one. States that showed US military involvement post-treaty were named Group two. The second step involved a detailed analytical comparison of both groups pre-treaty and post-treat to explore if proximity to the United States had significance in terms of US military involvement.

3.3 DATA COLLECTION

Quantitative research methods were not used because of the emphasis of the method in generalizing from a sample to the population. For this study, the entire population was examined using qualitative research, which considers complexity and multiple realities. This study was conducted to examine the complexities of US bilateral treaties states with other foreign states.

Data collection was consistent throughout the review of the historical literature on the topic. The information was interpreted using qualitative analysis, which was utilized for understanding patterns from the literature. This research was ideal for analyzing patterns of US military involvement in bilateral treaty states and its relationship with US military involvement. After the relationship was identified, a deeper examination was conducted to determine the factors that differentiated countries that showed an increase in military involvement post-treaty to countries that did not show an increase in military involvement, post-treaty.

3.3.1 DOCUMENT REVIEW

Document reviews can offer comprehensive and historical information necessary for the examination of US bilateral treaties. The validity of a qualitative study is present in studies, because qualitative study incorporates document reviews, which provide unbiased background data. Document review also provides the ability to study trends that are easy to analyze and utilize for the study performed. These forms of reviews offer substantiated findings that explain what happened, with whom, and what were the consequences and/or results.

3.4 TESTING THE ENTIRE POPULATION

There are three key benefits to being in a position where studying the entire population is possible. These benefits include faster data collection, higher accuracy, more control over the subjects, and easier to avoid error when inputting and analyzing data. The information gathered for this study came from seventeen US bilateral trade treaties. In this study, the entire population of US bilateral trade treaties was examined. These bilateral trade treaties comprised of all the states that the United States engaged and ratified trade treaties with around the world.

CHAPTER 4

ANALYSIS OF FINDINGS

The chapter is divided into several sections. The first section contains the historical overview of US bilateral trade treaties and US military involvement. The second section discusses the US bilateral trade treaties with foreign states that showed no increase in US military involvement post-treaty. The third section discusses the US bilateral trade treaties with foreign states that showed an increase in US military involvement post-treaty. The fourth section discusses the role of proximity in military involvement. The fifth section contains the limitations of the results.

4.1 HISTORY OF US BILATERAL TRADE TREATIES AND US MILITARY INVOLVEMENT

The following section will provide summative assessments of the history of US bilateral trade treaties and US military involvement since the eighteenth century.

4.1.1 EIGHTEENTH CENTURY

The history of United States engagement in these treaties with foreign states is rooted in the eighteenth century.[70] During this period, the Model Treaty was created to help guide US foreign relations and trade, which began the involvement of the United States with France and Spain to secure military assistance against the British during the American Revolution.[71] The Treaty of Alliance was established in 1776 and became the marking point of US military involvement with treaty states. US relations with foreign states continued throughout the late eighteenth century. In October 1782, the Continental Congress developed a Treaty of Amity and Commerce between the United States and Dutch Republic.[72] These alliances continued with Sweden when the United States signed the Treaty of Amity and Commerce on April 3, 1783.[73] The eighteenth century established how the United States used military power in treaties as a way to be in a better position to become an independent state and protect national security.

---

70 "Diplomatic History."
71 "Diplomatic History."
72 Israel, *The Dutch Republic.*
73 "Relationship between US and Swedish Militaries."

4.1.2 NINETEENTH CENTURY

The nineteenth century was no different in establishing relationships between the United States and foreign states. In 1833, the first formal treaty between the United States and the Kingdom of Siam was signed.[74] This treaty provided access to military facilities as well as military cooperation between both states, which enabled strategic US presence in the Asia-Pacific region.[75] After the treaty was ratified, the foundation of US and Asia-Pacific military relations was established, such as the US-Thailand treaty.[76] On July 3, 1844, the United States and China signed a diplomatic agreement known as the Treaty of Wang Hiya[77]. Since then, the United States has maintained military presence in China. Through the 1850s, the United States established the East Indies Squadron to support both China and Taiwan. The nineteenth solidified US treaty relationships to allow military involvement to protect the US national security as the United States expanded west.

4.1.3 TWENTIETH CENTURY

On November 18, 1901, the United States and the United Kingdom signed the Hay-Pauncefote Treaty, which gave the United States the power to create and control a canal across Central America to connect the Pacific Ocean and the Atlantic Ocean.[78]

In 1984, negotiations began between the United States and Israel. The trade was signed on April 22, 1985 with the purpose of lowering barriers to trade goods. The treaty became the first Free Trade Agreement for the United States. The twentieth century solidified the US treaty relations to allow military presence in Central America, while protecting trade throughout the Panama Canal. Securing this coast-to-coast was integral to the expansion of the United States in the West. Both the treaties in Central America and Israel helped protect US national security along the shores of the United States and strategic global locations.

4.1.4 TWENTY-FIRST CENTURY

The twenty-first century brought about a new age of technology, which necessitated new borders of protection that needed to be established by the United States. The United States have solidified treaty relations to allow military involvement. As the United States expanded technological reach around the world, relations with other states were formalized to protect the national security of the United States.

In 2001, the United States formed a bilateral trade agreement with Jordan, which was the first trade agreement of the United States with an Arab country.[79] The trade brought widespread

---

74   "Looking Back: A Brief History."

75   "Thailand: Background."

76   "Cobra Gold."

77   "China-US Trade Issues."

78   "US-UK Relations."

79   "US-Korea Free Trade Agreement: Potential Economy-Wide and Selected Sectoral Effects," last modified 2007. http://www.usitc.gov/publications/332/pub3949.pdf.

bipartisan and multisectoral support. Bilateral treaties with Australia, Chile, and Singapore shortly followed. The US-Australia trade agreement was passed in August 2004, and came into effect on January 1, 2005. The US-Chile trade agreement came into force on January 1, 2004. The trade with Singapore also came into force on January 1, 2004. By 2005, the United States had created trade agreements with Central America to eliminate tariffs. The United States established trade agreements with the Dominican Republic, Costa Rica, El Salvador, Guatemala, Honduras, and Nicaragua. In 2006, Bahrain, Morocco, and Oman established trade agreements with the United States. In 2007, the US-Peru bilateral trade agreement was implemented to eliminate obstacles to trade, consolidate access to goods and services, and foster private investment. The year of 2011 marked the US bilateral trade agreements between Panama, Colombia, and South Korea.

4.2 BILATERAL TREATIES WITH NO INCREASED US MILITARY INVOLVEMENT POST-TREATY

Out of the seventeen states that have bilateral trade treaties with the United States, eleven showed no increase in US military involvement post-treaty. This was further divided into two groups: Group one-A and Group one-B. Group one-A includes states that had zero military involvement pre-treaty and post-treaty. This sub-group includes Costa Rica, Guatemala, and Jordan. Group one-B includes states that had military involvement pre-treaty, but the extent of military involvement did not change post-treaty. This sub-group includes Dominican Republic, El Salvador, Honduras, Korea, Morocco, Nicaragua, Oman, and Singapore. This section contains discussions that provided insights about the factors that might have been significant in explaining why these bilateral treaty states showed no increase or change in US military involvement post-treaty.

4.2.1 GROUP ONE-A STATES

As stated in the preceding section, group one-A includes states that had zero military involvement pre-treaty and post-treaty. This sub-group includes Costa Rica, Guatemala, and Jordan.

Costa Rica. Pre-treaty, the United States had no military bases in Costa Rica. The treaty was an agreement that involved the elimination of tariffs to improve economic activities, opening up of markets, reduction of barriers to services, and the promotion of transparency between the participating countries. The treaty was revised in 2008 to change the agreement regarding the textile and apparel industry, specifically noting that textile used in apparel should originate from the participating countries only. After entering into the bilateral trade treaty with the United States, no changes in military involvement occurred in Costa Rica. The United States had no permanent US military personnel in Costa Rica, from pre-treaty until post-treaty.

Guatemala. Pre-treaty, the United States had no military bases in Guatemala. The treaty was an agreement that involved the elimination of tariffs to improve economic activities, opening up of markets, reduction of barriers to services, and the promotion of transparency between the participating countries. The treaty was revised in 2008 to change the agreement regarding the textile and apparel industry, specifically noting that textile used in apparel should originate from the participating countries only. No changes in military involvement occurred in Guatemala post-treaty. The United States had no permanent military personnel in Guatemala, from pre-treaty until post-treaty.

Jordan. The trade treaty between the United States and Jordan was created to the United States had no US military involvement in Jordan prior to entering into the bilateral trade treaty with the United States. No changes in military involvement occurred in Jordan post-treaty. The United States had no permanent US military personnel in Jordan, both pre-treaty and post-treaty.

4.2.2. GROUP ONE-B STATES

As stated previously, group one-B includes states that had military involvement pre-treaty, but the extent of military involvement did not change post-treaty. This sub-group includes Dominican Republic, El Salvador, Honduras, Korea, Morocco, Nicaragua, Oman, and Singapore.

Dominican Republic. The treaty between Dominican Republic and the United States involved the elimination of tariffs to improve economic activities, opening up of markets, reduction of barriers to services, and the promotion of transparency between the participating countries. The treaty was revised in 2008 to change the agreement regarding the textile and apparel industry, specifically noting that textile used in apparel should originate from the participating countries only. Pre-treaty, the United States had one military base in the Dominican Republic. The US military base was established in Samana in 1965, with 22,000 permanent military personnel in the Dominican Republic. The number of military bases in the Dominican Republic did not change post-treaty.

El Salvador. Pre-treaty, the United States had one military base in El Salvador. The military base for the US Air Force and Marines was established in 2000 in Comalapa. When a treaty was made in 2004 between the United States and El Salvador, the agreement involved the elimination of tariffs to improve economic activities, opening up of markets, reduction of barriers to services, and the promotion of transparency between the participating countries. The treaty was revised in 2008 to change the agreement regarding the textile and apparel industry, specifically noting that textile used in apparel should originate from the participating countries only. No changes in military involvement occurred in El Salvador post-treaty. El Salvador had 25 permanent US military personnel on the ground, from pre-treaty until post-treaty.

Honduras. The United States had one military base in Honduras, pre-treaty. The military base for the US Air Force was established in 1980 in Soto Cano. The treaty between Honduras and the United States in 2004 involved the elimination of tariffs to improve economic activities, opening up of markets, reduction of barriers to services, and the promotion of transparency between the participating countries. The treaty was revised in 2008 to change the agreement regarding the textile and apparel industry, specifically noting that textile used in apparel should originate from the participating countries only. No changes in military involvement occurred in Honduras post-treaty. The United States had 550 permanent US military personnel in Honduras, from pre-treaty until post-treaty.

Nicaragua. Pre-treaty, the United States had one military base in Nicaragua. The US Marine Military base was established in 1896 in the Port of Corinto, with 2,300 permanent military personnel. A treaty was created in 2004, wherein an agreement was made involving the elimination of tariffs to improve economic activities, opening up of markets, reduction of barriers to services, and the promotion of transparency between the participating countries. The treaty was revised in 2008 to change the agreement regarding the textile and apparel industry, specifically noting that textile used in apparel should originate from the participating countries only. No changes in military involvement occurred in Nicaragua post-treaty.

Korea. Pre-treaty, the United States had four military bases in Korea. A treaty between South Korea and the United States was created in 2007, and was amended in 2010, focusing on strengthening the auto manufacturing industry in both countries. The reduction and eventual elimination of tariffs in various sectors were also included in the trade treaty. No changes in military involvement occurred in Korea post-treaty, only maintaining the four existing bases pre-treaty. The United States had 28,500 permanent US military personnel in Korea, from pre-treaty until post-treaty.

Morocco. Pre-treaty, the United States had two military bases in Morocco. The first of the two bases was the US Air Force Strategic Air Command (SAC) in Nouasseur Air Base, which was established in 1951. The other base was the US Navy in Naval Air Station Port Lyautey, which was established in 1977 in Kenitra. The United States had 2,700 permanent US military personnel in Morocco, from pre-treaty until post-treaty.

Oman. Pre-treaty, the United States had two military bases in Oman. The first military base was established in 1980 in Masirah Air Base, on the East Coast of Oman. The next year, the US Air Force in Seeb International Airport was established. No changes in military involvement occurred in Oman post-treaty. The United States had 3,000 permanent military personnel in Oman, from pre-treaty until post-treaty.[80]

Singapore. Pre-treaty, the United States had two military bases in Singapore. The US Navy Military base was established in Sembawang in 1992. The second base was the US Air Force Base (497th Combat Training Squadron) in PayaLebar Air Base, which was established in 1990. No changes in military involvement occurred in Singapore post-treaty. The United States had 180 permanent military personnel in Singapore, from pre-treaty until post-treaty.[81]

---

[80]   "Bahrain: Reform."

[81]   "Thailand: Background."

4.3 BILATERAL TREATIES WITH INCREASED US MILITARY INVOLVEMENT POST-TREATY

Six out of the seventeen US bilateral trade treaty states showed an increase in military involvement post-treaty. These states are: Australia, Bahrain, Chile, Colombia, Israel, and Peru. Colombia was the only country wherein the United States already had military involvement pre-treaty. This section is important to show the possible factors that might have been significant in explaining why these treaty states showed an increase or change in US military involvement post-treaty. When the pre-treaty and post-treaty conditions of the six states were compared, all six states showed an increase in US military bases and troops.

4.3.1 AUSTRALIA

Pre-treaty, the United States had no military presence in Australia. After the bilateral trade treaty was made on January 1, 2005, the United States established the Darwin's Robertson Barracks US Marine Base in 2011 to create strategic military alliances against uncertain Chinese military intentions.[82] The United States and Australia trade agreement allowed the relation between both states to evolve, allowing Australia to create an alliance with the United States after China's global military threat to the state. The United States had no permanent US military personnel in Australia pre-treaty, but 1,000 permanent US military troops were established post-treaty. This base has become the United States Pacific Command for Marine deployment and has a capacity of 4,500 troops.[83]

4.3.2 BAHRAIN

Pre-treaty, the United States had no military presence in Bahrain. A bilateral trade treaty was put into effect on January 11, 2006, wherein US farmers are able to export their products to Bahrain. For Bahrain, the benefits of the trade treaty were both economic and political in nature. Post-treaty, the United States established two new bases in Bahrain to provide critical mission support and dependable access to the Persian Gulf, and to provide support to aerial port operations.[84] The United States had no permanent US military personnel in Bahrain pre-treaty, but 2,000 permanent US military troops were stationed in Bahrain post-treaty.

4.3.3 CHILE

Pre-treaty, the United States had no military presence in Chile. Post-treaty, the United States established one military base in 2012 in Concon, the US Southern Command. The United States claimed that the base will be used to train forces in peacekeeping operations. Chile had

---

[82]   "US Marines to Darwin, Australia: Evolution of an Idea," last modified November 18, 2011.http://cogitasia.com/u-s-marines-to-darwin-australia-evolution-of-an-idea/.

[83]   "US Marines in Darwin."

[84]   "Bahrain: Reform."

no permanent US military personnel on the ground pre-treaty, but 100 permanent US military troops are on the ground post-treaty.

4.3.4 COLOMBIA

Pre-treaty, the United States had two US military bases in Colombia. The bases were the US Army Base at Melgar Air Base in Melgar, Tolima, and the US military base in La Macarena, Meta.[85] Post-treaty, the United States established eight new bases, which included the Cartagena Naval Base, the Malambo Air Base, the Tolemaida Air Base in Barranquilla, the Apiay Air Base in Melgar, Tolima, the Malaga Naval Base in Meta, Bahia, the San Jose del Guaviare Radar Station in Buenaventura, the Marandua Radar Station, and the Leticia Radar Station.[86] The United States had 10,000 permanent US military personnel on the ground pre-treaty, and 2,000 permanent US military troops were added post-treaty.

4.3.5 ISRAEL

Pre-treaty, the United States had no military presence in Israel. Post-treaty, the United States established three new bases: US Navy Sixth Fleet Military Base in Port Haifa, Dimona Radar Facility, and a radar base in Negev.[87] The United States had no permanent US military personnel in Israel pre-treaty, but 120 permanent US military troops were established in Israel post-treaty.

4.3.6 PERU

Pre-treaty, the United States had no military presence in Peru. Post-treaty, the United States established two military bases: the US Navy and US Air Force base in Lima in 2003, and a US radar Installation in Lima. The United States had no permanent US military personnel in Peru pre-treaty, but 200 permanent US military troops were established post-treaty.[88]

4.4 THE ROLE OF PROXIMITY IN MILITARY INVOLVEMENT

When comparing the geographical proximity of the United States to both Group one (both Group one-A and Group one-B) and Group two states (including Colombia), there was no indication that proximity played a significant role in increasing US military involvement. These conclusions were based on comparing the geographical proximity of every state that had bilateral trade treaty with the United States. In Group one states, the geographical proximity in miles ranged from 1511.64 (Guatemala) to 9511.35 (Singapore). The wide range of states included in Group one, which included countries from South America to Asia, suggest that proximity had

---

[85] "Pentagon Building Bases."

[86] "Pentagon Building Bases."

[87] "Port of Haifa Study."

[88] "Pentagon Build Bases."

no role in the lack of changes in military involvement of the United States, post-treaty. Figure 1 shows the geographic proximity of all the Group one states to the United States.

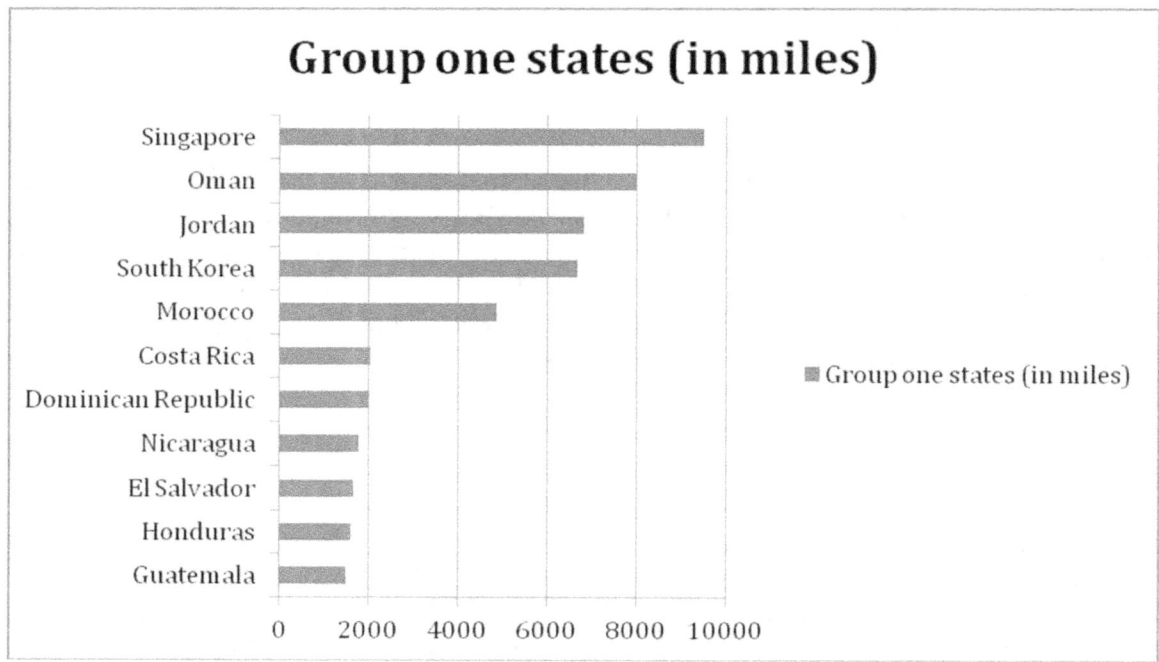

Figure 1: Proximity of group one states from the United States

Similar to the Group one states, the group two states, including Colombia, also did not show any clear pattern about the role of geographic proximity in the increase of military involvement of the United States post-treaty. In Group two states, the geographical proximity in miles ranged from 2626.56 (Colombia) to 9477.77 (Australia). The wide range of states included in Group two, which included countries from South America to Asia, suggest that proximity had no role in the changes in military involvement of the United States in these countries, post-treaty. Figure 2 shows the geographic proximity of all the Group two states to the United States.

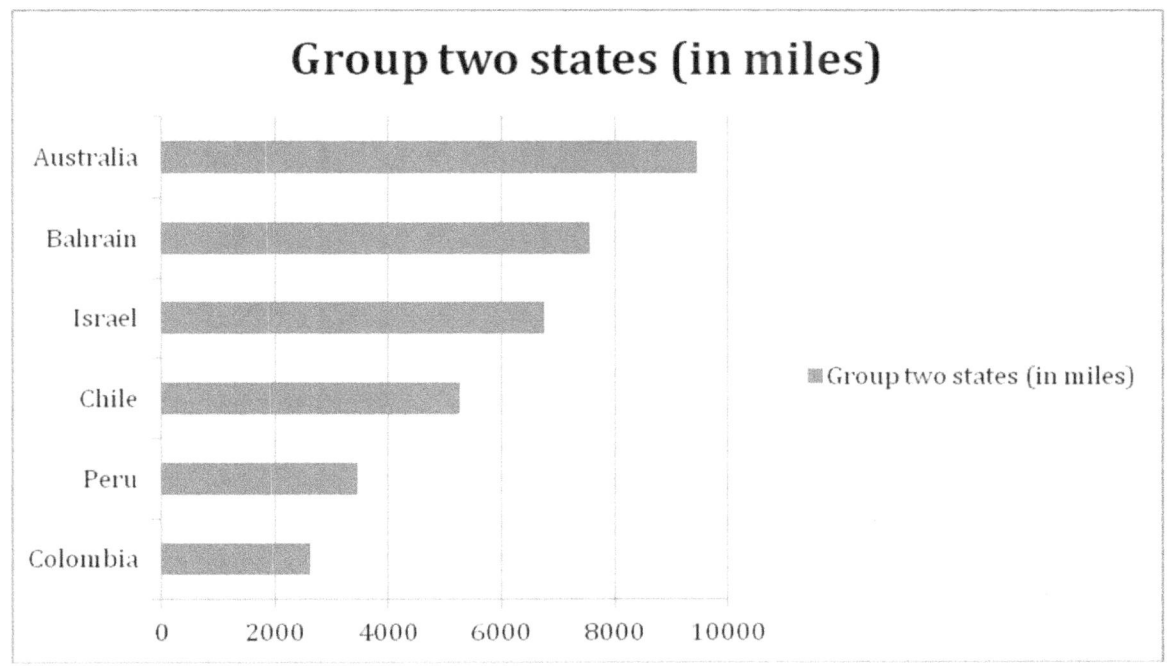

Figure 2: Proximity of group two states from the United States

The distance between the United States and Australia is 9477.77 miles. In the case of the US-Australia bilateral trade treaty, two military bases were added after the bilateral treaty was ratified. The distance between the United States and Bahrain is 7562.21 miles. There was an increase of two US military bases post-treaty. The distance between the United States and Israel is 6755.68 miles. In the case of the US-Israel bilateral trade treaty, two military bases were added after the bilateral treaty was ratified. The distance between the United States and Chile is 5266.949 miles. In the case of the US-Chile bilateral trade treaty, three military bases were added after the bilateral treaty was ratified. The distance between the United States and Peru is 3471.344 miles. There was an increase of six US military bases post-treaty. The distance between the United States and Colombia is 6755.677 miles. In the case of the US-Colombia bilateral trade treaty, eight military bases were added after the bilateral treaty was ratified.

When the distance of all the countries in Group one was added together, the average distance between Group one states and the United States is 4251.15 miles. For the Group two states, the average distance between Group two states and the United States is 5860.06 miles. Figure 3 shows the average distance of Group one and two states from the United States.

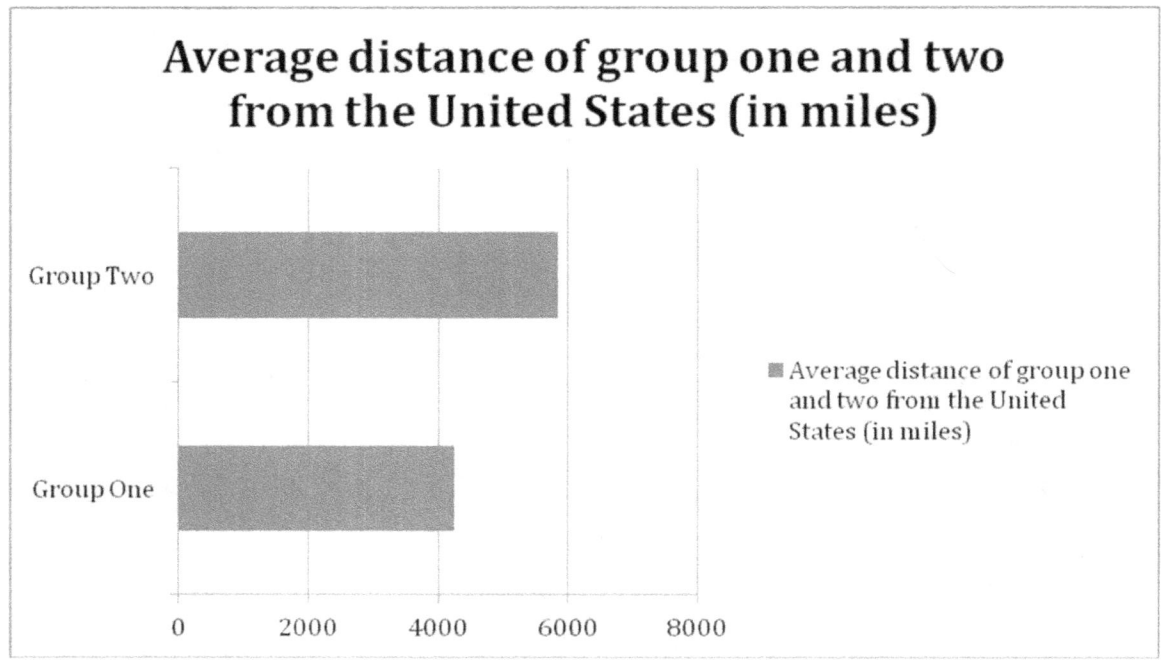

Figure 3: Average distance of group one and two from the United States

Based on the data presented above (Figures 1-3), it appears that proximity had no influence on whether military involvement of the United States in foreign countries that are part of bilateral treaties would increase post-treaty. This conclusion was arrived at based on the lack of homogeneity for each of two groups that were compared. In both Groups one and two, there was no consistent trend about the distance of the countries from the United States. Each group had countries from South America to Asia, and other parts of the world, suggesting that geographical proximity had no significant role in increasing military involvement post-trade treaty.

4.5 COMPARING THE IMPORTS AND EXPORTS OF GROUP ONE AND GROUP TWO STATES

In this section, the average import and export for both Group one and two is analyzed. Data gained from this analysis was used to differentiate the two groups, one group did not show an increase in US military involvement post-treaty (Group one), whereas the other group showed an increase in US military involvement post-treaty (Group two). To compare the import and export of countries pre-treaty and post-treaty, data five years before the ratification of trade treaty and five years after the ratification of trade treaty were compared.

4.5.1 IMPORTS

Based on the data available, all of the countries in Group one states showed an increase in the import of goods post-treaty, except for the Dominican Republic. Among the Group one states, Jordan had the highest increase in import post-treaty, with an increase of 2,748%. The

Dominican Republic had a decrease of 9.17% in the import of goods from the United States post-treaty. Table 1 shows the complete data for the average import of good in millions pre-treaty and post-treaty.

Table 1: Average import pre-treaty and post-treaty (group one)

	PRE-TREATY (Import)	POST-TREATY (Import)	PERCENTAGE OF CHANGE
Costa Rica	3,252.8	5,206.5	60.06% increase
Dominican Republic	4,343.6	3,945.4	9.17% decrease
El Salvador	1,973.5	2,031.1	2.92% increase
Guatemala	2,818.7	3,186.3	13.04% increase
Honduras	3,286.1	3,748.5	15.17% increase
Nicaragua	720.3	1,690.6	134.69% increase
South Korea	45,905.0	58,879.0	19.55% increase
Singapore	12,827.3	16,572.3	29.29% increase
Oman	497.7	1,156.4	132.26% increase
Morocco	434.6	727.5	67.38% increase
Jordan	34.9	973.6	2,748.57% increase
TOTAL	76,094.5	98,117.2	28.94% increase

Note: All numbers are in millions

All group two states showed an increase in the import of goods from the United States post-treaty. Among the Group two states, Chile had the highest increase in import post-treaty, at 162.59%. Bahrain had the lowest increase in import post-treaty, with only 26.13%. Table 2 shows the complete data for the average import of good in millions pre-treaty and post-treaty for Group two states.

Table 2: Average import pre-treaty and post-treaty (group two)

	PRE-TREATY (Import)	POST-TREATY (Import)	PERCENTAGE OF CHANGE
Chile	2,995.8	7,874.4	162.59% increase
Peru	3,809.4	5,624.2	47.64% increase
Colombia	11,754	24,632	109.56% increase
Bahrain	406.4	512.6	26.13% increase
Israel	N/A	2,600.6	N/A
Australia	6,217.2	8,552	37.55% increase
TOTAL	24,776.4	49,795.8	100% increase

Note: Numbers are in millions. The total post-treaty import for Israel was not included in the calculations.

The results of the analysis showed that the average percentage of increase in imports post-treaty was 28.94% in Group one states, whereas 100% was the increase in the Group two states. This indicates that Group two states, which all showed an increase in military involvement post-treaty, had higher average import of goods from the United States.

4.5.2 EXPORTS

Based on the data available, all of the countries in Group one states showed an increase in the export of goods post-treaty. Among the Group one states, Morocco had the highest increase in export post-treaty, with an increase of 298%. El Salvador showed the least increase in the export of goods from the United States post-treaty, with only 27.99% increase. Table 3 shows the complete data for the average export of good in millions pre-treaty and post-treaty.

Table 3: Average export pre-treaty and post-treaty (group one)

	PRE-TREATY (Export)	POST-TREATY (Export)	PERCENTAGE OF CHANGE
Costa Rica	2,959.4	4,854.0	64.04% increase
Dominican Republic	4,336.4	5,975.0	37.79% increase
El Salvador	1,778	2,275.6	27.99% increase
Guatemala	2,125.4	4,129.2	94.27% increase
Honduras	2,694	4,393.4	63.08% increase
Nicaragua	470.6	886.2	88.31% increase
South Korea	35,176.8	N/A	N/A
Singapore	16,896.2	23,998.6	42.04% increase
Oman	834.1	1428.6	71.27% increase
Morocco	458.4	1,825.6	298.25% increase
Jordan	338.2	548.2	62.09% increase
TOTAL	32,890.7	50,313.8	52.97% increase

Note: all numbers in millions. Korea was not included in the calculations.

All group two states showed an increase in the export of good from the United States post-treaty. Among the Group two states, Chile had the highest increase in export post-treaty, at 128.82%. Bahrain had the lowest increase in export post-treaty, with only 26.15%. Table 4 shows the complete data for the average export of good in millions pre-treaty and post-treaty for Group two states.

Table 4: Average export pre-treaty and post-treaty (group two)

	PRE-TREATY (Export)	POST-TREATY (Export)	PERCENTAGE OF CHANGE
Chile	3,441.5	7,874.7	128.82% increase
Peru	3,809.8	5,624.8	47.64% increase
Colombia	11,755.0	24,632.4	109.55% increase
Bahrain	406.8	513.1	26.15% increase
Israel	N/A	2,601.0	N/A
Australia	6,217.7	8,552.3	37.55% increase
TOTAL	25,630.8	47,197.3	84.14% increase

Note: Numbers are in millions. The total post-treaty export for Israel was not included in the calculations.

The results of the analysis showed that the average percentage of increase in exports post-treaty was 52.97% in Group one states, whereas 84.14% was the increase in the Group two states. This indicates that Group two states, which all showed an increase in military involvement post-treaty, had higher average export of goods to the United States.

4.6 COMPARING THE IMPORTS AND EXPORTS OF GROUP ONE-A AND GROUP TWO STATES

The previous section contained a comparison of all the states in each of the groups. To have a more focused comparison of imports and exports of the groups in the study, Group one-A and Group two (excluding Colombia) states were compared. The United States had no military involvement in Group one-A states pre-treaty and post-treaty. In order to compare the import and export of countries pre-treaty and post-treaty, data five years before the ratification of trade treaty and five years after the ratification of trade treaty were compared.

4.6.1 IMPORTS

Based on the data available, all of the countries in Group one-A states showed an increase in the import of goods post-treaty. The average percentage of the increase in import was 53.39%. Table 5 shows the complete data for the average import of good in millions pre-treaty and post-treaty for Group one-A states.

Table 5: Average import pre-treaty and post-treaty (group one-A)

	PRE-TREATY (Import)	POST-TREATY (Import)	PERCENTAGE OF CHANGE
Costa Rica	3,252.8	5,206.5	60.06% increase
Guatemala	2,818.7	3,186.3	13.04% increase
Jordan	34.9	973.6	2,748.57% increase
TOTAL	6,106.4	9,366.4	53.39% increase

Note: All numbers are in millions

All group two states showed an increase in the import of goods from the United States post-treaty. The average percentage of increase in import for the group was 68.02%. Table 6 shows the complete data for the average import of good in millions pre-treaty and post-treaty for Group two states.

Table 6: Average import pre-treaty and post-treaty (group two—w/o Colombia)

	PRE-TREATY (Import)	POST-TREATY (Import)	PERCENTAGE OF CHANGE
Chile	2,995.8	7,874.4	162.59% increase
Peru	3,809.4	5,624.2	47.64% increase
Bahrain	406.4	512.6	26.13% increase
Israel	N/A	2,600.6	N/A
Australia	6,217.2	8,552	37.55% increase
TOTAL	13,428.8	22,563.2	68.02% increase

Note: Numbers are in millions. The total post-treaty import for Israel was not included in the calculations.

The results of the analysis showed that the average percentage of increase in imports post-treaty was 53.39% in Group one-A states, whereas 68.02% was the increase in the Group two states. This indicates that Group two states, which all showed an increase in military involvement post-treaty, had higher average import of goods from the United States.

4.6.2 EXPORTS

Based on the data available, all of the countries in Group one-A showed an increase in the export of goods post-treaty. The average change in the percentage of export was 75.76%. Table 7 shows the complete data for the average export of good in millions pre-treaty and post-treaty.

Table 7: Average export pre-treaty and post-treaty (group one-A)

	PRE-TREATY (Export)	POST-TREATY (Export)	PERCENTAGE OF CHANGE
Costa Rica	2,959.4	4,854.0	64.04% increase
Guatemala	2,125.4	4,129.2	94.27% increase
Jordan	338.2	548.2	62.09% increase
TOTAL	5,423	9,531.4	75.76% increase

Note: all numbers in millions.

All group two states showed an increase in the export of goods from the United States post-treaty. The average change in the percentage of export was 67.53%. Table 8 shows the complete data for the average export of good in millions pre-treaty and post-treaty for Group two states.

Table 8: Average export pre-treaty and post-treaty (group two—w/o Colombia)

	PRE-TREATY (Export)	POST-TREATY (Export)	PERCENTAGE OF CHANGE
Chile	3,441.5	7,874.7	128.82% increase
Peru	3,809.8	5,624.8	47.64% increase
Bahrain	406.8	513.1	26.15% increase
Israel	N/A	2,601.0	N/A
Australia	6,217.7	8,552.3	37.55% increase
TOTAL	13,469	22,564.9	67.53% increase

Note: Numbers are in millions. The total post-treaty export for Israel was not included in the calculations.

The results of the analysis showed that the average percentage of increase in exports post-treaty was 75.76% in Group one-A states, whereas 67.53% was the increase in the Group two states. This indicates that Group one-A states, which all did not show an increase in military involvement post-treaty, had higher average export of goods to the United States.

4.7 LIMITATIONS

There were three major limitations to this study. First, the sample size was small. The seventeen states that comprised the sample may not have been able to represent the majority of the states that have bilateral trade relations with other states. Second, the reliability of the findings may not be a clear representation of the world. In addition, because the researcher conducted the assessment of the pre-test and post-test, some degree of subjectivity may have been exercised. Third, even though there were differences observed in the groups that were compared, the researcher was not able to determine if they were statistically significant. These limitations are expanded upon in the subsequent sub-sections.

4.7.1 SAMPLE SIZE

Even though the sample size for this study involved the entire population of US bilateral trade treaties, the sample size can still be considered small. A normal sample of thirty is preferred when conducting a study. Due to the lack of bilateral trade treaties between the United States and other foreign states, only seventeen cases were assembled for this study. The limited sample size and variability may have affected the results.

4.7.2 RELIABILITY AND VALIDITY

Public information, particularly when dealing with military information, can be very limited. Relations between states and military involvement are considered sensitive information, making the process of collecting data difficult to the general public. The establishment of a military base in a foreign state has a specific purpose, and one of the reasons could be to protect the foreign country from invasion from other countries. In such cases, information has to be kept confidential, thus limiting information to the public.

Public information is limited when dealing with military involvement; accessibility to detailed and accurate information can become a challenge. The details of US military bases were limited in information, such as date of establishment, exact locations, and number of personnel, because of reasons linked to confidentiality and liability. Therefore, there was a limitation in the accessibility of information that was of a true reliable source. Speculations and rumored information were abundant, which caused a limitation in deciphering the veracity of the information used in this study.

4.7.3 STATISTICAL SIGNIFICANCE

Another limitation pertained to the statistical significance of the differences that were observed between the groups that were compared. This study was qualitative in nature wherein historical data were analyzed and compared. Even though a component of the historical data used in the analysis involved numbers, statistical analysis was not performed in this study. The comparisons that were made were based on qualitative interpretations of the data, limiting the definitiveness of the conclusions made in this study. This study is limited by not using statistical tools in the comparison of the data from the different groups.

CHAPTER 5

CONCLUSIONS

The aim of this research was to examine the factors that differentiated the countries that showed an increase in military involvement of the United States in foreign states compared to countries that did not show an increase in military involvement of the United States in foreign states. This chapter is organized into two sections: conclusions and recommendations. The conclusions contain the discussion of the findings. Based on the findings, several recommendations are proposed.

5.1 CONCLUSIONS

For the study, the seventeen US bilateral trade treaty states examined were divided into two groups. Group one included Costa Rica, the Dominican Republic, El Salvador, Guatemala, Honduras, Jordan, Korea, Morocco, Nicaragua, Oman, and Singapore. In Group one, the evidence showed no increase in US military involvement in foreign treaty states when military involvement was compared pre-treaty and post-treaty. Group two includes Australia, Bahrain, Chile, Colombia, Israel, and Peru. In Group two, the evidence showed an increase in US military involvement in foreign treaty states when military involvement was compared pre-treaty and post-treaty. The US military involvement showed an increase in both military bases and permanent US military troops in Group two states.

The results of the study showed that post-treaty, both Group one and Group two states experienced higher import and export. However, the results indicate that the percentage of increase for both import and export were higher in Group two states compared to Group one states. The higher percentage of import and export in Group two states is a differentiating factor from Group one states, which could be significant in explaining the increase of military involvement in Group two states post-treaty.

To control for the differences in the pre-treaty conditions of both Group one and group two states, the groups were further stratified. Group one-A (states that had no military involvement from the United States pre-treaty and post-treaty) and group two states (excluding Colombia) were compared and analyzed to examine if differences exist. The results revealed that trade treaties of the United States with foreign states that showed an increase in military involvement post-treaty reflected higher imports but lower exports compared to countries that had trade treaties with the United States that showed no increase in military involvement post-treaty. The findings suggest that when trade is more beneficial to the bilateral trade partner of the United States, as reflected by higher import and lower export, increased military involvement of the United States could be a result. Even though several factors could also contribute to the differences in military involvement between the groups, the results suggest the significance of trade, as reflected by the average import and export of the United States with their trade partners.

The findings were further analyzed to examine if proximity played any role in US military involvement. The hypothesis that proximity played a role in the increase of military involvement post-treaty was disproven in this study. There was no indication that proximity had any significant role in the increase of military involvement of the United States in Group two states post-treaty. The results show that, among the states in Group one, proximity was not a significant factor in US military involvement post-treaty. There was no increase in US military involvement among the eleven states in Group one. The findings showed that among the states in Group two, proximity also did not play a role in the increase in US military involvement post-treaty.

Based on the findings, the following conclusions are made:

1. Bilateral trade treaties resulted in increased imports and exports of goods between the United States and both Group one and Group two states.
2. Group two states (excluding Colombia), which all had an increase in US military involvement post-treaty, had higher increase in import but lower increase in export post-treaty. This differentiated Group two states (excluding Colombia) from Group one-A states.
3. For both Group one and two states, proximity did not play a role in increasing US military involvement post-treaty.

5.2 RECOMMENDATIONS

Upon reflection of the results, proximity appears to be not a significant factor in the increase of military involvement of the United States in foreign countries post-treaty. This is not consistent with the literature reviewed, which suggests that proximity could have a role in increased military involvement of the United States. Because the study only involved a small sample of seventeen states, the significance of proximity cannot be generalized in a larger population. Other researchers should expand the scope of the sample to verify the findings of this study.

Confidential information regarding military personnel and bases was not accessible. The true objectives and behavioral patterns of the US military remain inaccessible at some level, which makes the topic difficult to study. As more information becomes declassified, future studies should examine the impact of this new information on bilateral trade treaties and military involvement. Other research may be able to identify a measurable point to distinguish the importance of US military involvement as a result of entering a bilateral trade treaty with a foreign state.

The results of the study expanded the literature on military involvement as a result of bilateral trade treaties. The more complex challenges involved assessing the impact of US bilateral trade treaties, US military involvement, and proximity. Future studies could further advance these points by examining the sociological and cultural component of US bilateral trade treaties, military involvement, and proximity. These new studies might involve innovative ways to present new approaches to the problem identified in this study.

APPENDIX

DATA TABLES

2000 : U.S. trade in goods with Costa Rica

NOTE: All figures are in millions of U.S. dollars on a nominal basis, not seasonally adjusted unless otherwise specified. Details may not equal totals due to rounding.

Month	Exports	Imports	Balance
January 2000	183.3	259.1	-75.8
February 2000	181.7	315.3	-133.6
March 2000	232.1	350.8	-118.7
April 2000	197.9	283.4	-85.5
May 2000	205.6	320.6	-115.0
June 2000	216.5	377.2	-160.7
July 2000	197.5	283.5	-86.0
August 2000	206.3	273.2	-66.9
September 2000	210.7	279.5	-68.8
October 2000	212.3	274.0	-61.7
November 2000	204.1	260.3	-56.2
December 2000	212.3	261.7	-49.4
TOTAL 2000	2,460.3	3,538.6	-1,078.3

2001 : U.S. trade in goods with Costa Rica

NOTE: All figures are in millions of U.S. dollars on a nominal basis, not seasonally adjusted unless otherwise specified. Details may not equal totals due to rounding.

Month	Exports	Imports	Balance
January 2001	207.2	205.5	1.7
February 2001	182.9	229.5	-46.6
March 2001	236.4	258.5	-22.1
April 2001	213.8	228.3	-14.5
May 2001	204.3	261.3	-57.0
June 2001	209.5	268.3	-58.8
July 2001	205.0	241.6	-36.6
August 2001	210.4	244.1	-33.7
September 2001	175.0	241.3	-66.3
October 2001	218.6	235.6	-17.0
November 2001	229.6	250.3	-20.7
December 2001	209.6	221.9	-12.3
TOTAL 2001	2,502.3	2,886.2	-383.9

2002 : U.S. trade in goods with Costa Rica

NOTE: All figures are in millions of U.S. dollars on a nominal basis, not seasonally adjusted unless otherwise specified. Details may not equal totals due to rounding.

Month	Exports	Imports	Balance
January 2002	201.1	188.1	13.0
February 2002	215.8	232.4	-16.6
March 2002	265.1	257.2	7.9
April 2002	244.6	250.5	-5.9
May 2002	262.7	275.9	-13.2
June 2002	268.5	276.7	-8.2
July 2002	270.3	282.4	-12.1
August 2002	337.9	275.0	62.9
September 2002	256.8	282.0	-25.2
October 2002	244.5	283.9	-39.4
November 2002	268.2	278.3	-10.1
December 2002	281.0	259.5	21.5
TOTAL 2002	3,116.5	3,141.9	-25.4

2003 : U.S. trade in goods with Costa Rica

NOTE: All figures are in millions of U.S. dollars on a nominal basis, not seasonally adjusted unless otherwise specified. Details may not equal totals due to rounding.

Month	Exports	Imports	Balance
January 2003	357.9	253.7	104.2
February 2003	307.2	286.0	21.2
March 2003	330.7	307.5	23.1
April 2003	276.7	276.3	0.4
May 2003	253.5	302.0	-48.5
June 2003	251.0	299.2	-48.2
July 2003	267.5	304.7	-37.2
August 2003	270.6	257.8	12.8
September 2003	291.8	271.8	19.9
October 2003	274.0	278.3	-4.3
November 2003	259.2	263.5	-4.3
December 2003	273.6	263.4	10.1
TOTAL 2003	3,413.5	3,364.2	49.3

2004 : U.S. trade in goods with Costa Rica

NOTE: All figures are in millions of U.S. dollars on a nominal basis, not seasonally adjusted unless otherwise specified. Details may not equal totals due to rounding.

Month	Exports	Imports	Balance
January 2004	281.5	213.8	67.7
February 2004	296.9	287.5	9.4
March 2004	338.3	329.4	8.9
April 2004	296.8	279.4	17.3
May 2004	293.4	296.2	-2.8
June 2004	280.2	314.6	-34.4
July 2004	289.3	271.1	18.3
August 2004	266.4	267.6	-1.2
September 2004	237.3	268.4	-31.1
October 2004	257.6	285.7	-28.1
November 2004	242.6	265.5	-22.9
December 2004	225.5	254.1	-28.6
TOTAL 2004	**3,305.9**	**3,333.3**	**-27.4**

2006 : U.S. trade in goods with Costa Rica

NOTE: All figures are in millions of U.S. dollars on a nominal basis, not seasonally adjusted unless otherwise specified. Details may not equal totals due to rounding.

Month	Exports	Imports	Balance
January 2006	316.2	265.1	51.1
February 2006	316.8	292.6	24.2
March 2006	339.9	404.5	-64.6
April 2006	365.3	288.5	76.9
May 2006	357.2	366.0	-8.7
June 2006	349.6	380.5	-30.8
July 2006	339.6	302.6	37.0
August 2006	335.0	321.7	13.3
September 2006	363.1	295.9	67.2
October 2006	357.8	303.7	54.2
November 2006	359.7	331.5	28.3
December 2006	332.1	291.9	40.2
TOTAL 2006	**4,132.4**	**3,844.1**	**288.2**

2007 : U.S. trade in goods with Costa Rica

NOTE: All figures are in millions of U.S. dollars on a nominal basis, not seasonally adjusted unless otherwise specified. Details may not equal totals due to rounding.

Month	Exports	Imports	Balance
January 2007	387.9	269.6	118.3
February 2007	365.6	308.3	57.3
March 2007	350.2	390.7	-40.6
April 2007	321.9	324.9	-3.0
May 2007	356.2	383.3	-27.1
June 2007	344.9	359.1	-14.2
July 2007	294.2	328.3	-34.1
August 2007	361.0	334.6	26.4
September 2007	387.7	298.7	89.0
October 2007	470.5	328.4	142.1
November 2007	517.8	325.0	192.7
December 2007	422.7	290.7	132.0
TOTAL 2007	4,580.5	3,941.5	638.9

2008 : U.S. trade in goods with Costa Rica

NOTE: All figures are in millions of U.S. dollars on a nominal basis, not seasonally adjusted unless otherwise specified. Details may not equal totals due to rounding.

Month	Exports	Imports	Balance
January 2008	421.9	303.5	118.4
February 2008	488.7	350.7	138.0
March 2008	427.7	359.0	68.7
April 2008	462.7	338.6	124.1
May 2008	492.6	371.8	120.8
June 2008	448.8	355.5	93.3
July 2008	526.2	358.3	167.9
August 2008	521.7	331.7	190.1
September 2008	528.7	332.5	196.2
October 2008	526.4	308.6	217.8
November 2008	451.2	256.6	194.6
December 2008	383.3	271.4	111.8
TOTAL 2008	5,679.8	3,938.1	1,741.8

2009 : U.S. trade in goods with Costa Rica

NOTE: All figures are in millions of U.S. dollars on a nominal basis, not seasonally adjusted unless otherwise specified. Details may not equal totals due to rounding.

Month	Exports	Imports	Balance
January 2009	353.5	225.8	127.8
February 2009	337.5	256.6	81.0
March 2009	327.3	284.7	42.7
April 2009	324.1	291.5	32.6
May 2009	393.9	291.4	102.5
June 2009	415.4	486.0	-70.6
July 2009	384.5	660.0	-275.5
August 2009	413.2	552.2	-138.9
September 2009	399.3	606.1	-206.8
October 2009	438.3	670.7	-232.5
November 2009	481.3	676.2	-194.9
December 2009	431.0	610.5	-179.5
TOTAL 2009	4,699.5	5,611.6	-912.1

2010 : U.S. trade in goods with Costa Rica

NOTE: All figures are in millions of U.S. dollars on a nominal basis, not seasonally adjusted unless otherwise specified. Details may not equal totals due to rounding.

Month	Exports	Imports	Balance
January 2010	406.3	580.1	-173.8
February 2010	421.6	535.7	-114.1
March 2010	465.1	816.7	-351.6
April 2010	478.8	629.6	-150.8
May 2010	483.3	735.2	-252.0
June 2010	420.8	747.5	-326.7
July 2010	411.6	685.7	-274.1
August 2010	375.5	801.9	-426.4
September 2010	438.2	888.5	-450.3
October 2010	431.7	730.8	-299.0
November 2010	460.3	769.2	-309.0
December 2010	386.7	776.2	-389.6
TOTAL 2010	5,179.7	8,697.2	-3,517.5

2000 : U.S. trade in goods with Dominican Republic

NOTE: All figures are in millions of U.S. dollars on a nominal basis, not seasonally adjusted unless otherwise specified. Details may not equal totals due to rounding.

Month	Exports	Imports	Balance
January 2000	297.0	178.9	118.1
February 2000	351.1	351.0	0.1
March 2000	412.8	414.2	-1.4
April 2000	388.6	327.1	61.5
May 2000	355.1	370.2	-15.1
June 2000	405.2	409.2	-4.0
July 2000	363.0	384.5	-21.5
August 2000	389.7	422.5	-32.8
September 2000	395.9	410.2	-14.3
October 2000	389.5	404.9	-15.4
November 2000	392.9	392.9	0.0
December 2000	332.0	317.7	14.3
TOTAL 2000	**4,472.8**	**4,383.3**	**89.5**

2001 : U.S. trade in goods with Dominican Republic

NOTE: All figures are in millions of U.S. dollars on a nominal basis, not seasonally adjusted unless otherwise specified. Details may not equal totals due to rounding.

Month	Exports	Imports	Balance
January 2001	339.7	252.0	87.7
February 2001	367.9	324.3	43.6
March 2001	409.0	386.4	22.6
April 2001	419.5	329.1	90.4
May 2001	376.4	373.6	2.8
June 2001	404.3	355.9	48.4
July 2001	326.9	372.3	-45.4
August 2001	371.0	385.8	-14.8
September 2001	334.5	350.1	-15.6
October 2001	379.7	386.6	-6.9
November 2001	346.9	350.5	-3.6
December 2001	321.6	316.8	4.8
TOTAL 2001	4,397.4	4,183.4	214.0

2002 : U.S. trade in goods with Dominican Republic

NOTE: All figures are in millions of U.S. dollars on a nominal basis, not seasonally adjusted unless otherwise specified. Details may not equal totals due to rounding.

Month	Exports	Imports	Balance
January 2002	314.3	194.5	119.8
February 2002	333.8	312.3	21.5
March 2002	365.3	333.9	31.4
April 2002	371.1	332.2	38.9
May 2002	387.0	379.8	7.2
June 2002	347.0	365.9	-18.9
July 2002	363.0	390.8	-27.8
August 2002	377.6	372.4	5.2
September 2002	351.9	378.7	-26.8
October 2002	379.2	396.4	-17.2
November 2002	347.7	355.6	-7.9
December 2002	312.2	356.3	-44.1
TOTAL 2002	4,250.1	4,168.8	81.3

2003 : U.S. trade in goods with Dominican Republic

NOTE: All figures are in millions of U.S. dollars on a nominal basis, not seasonally adjusted unless otherwise specified. Details may not equal totals due to rounding.

Month	Exports	Imports	Balance
January 2003	360.4	225.7	134.7
February 2003	347.2	336.0	11.2
March 2003	377.5	388.3	-10.8
April 2003	355.8	383.7	-27.9
May 2003	360.7	403.9	-43.2
June 2003	325.1	386.3	-61.1
July 2003	362.9	411.7	-48.8
August 2003	344.4	361.6	-17.3
September 2003	337.8	385.6	-47.8
October 2003	394.6	427.5	-32.9
November 2003	343.6	333.0	10.6
December 2003	295.4	411.9	-116.5
TOTAL 2003	**4,205.4**	**4,455.2**	**-249.8**

2004 : U.S. trade in goods with Dominican Republic

NOTE: All figures are in millions of U.S. dollars on a nominal basis, not seasonally adjusted unless otherwise specified. Details may not equal totals due to rounding.

Month	Exports	Imports	Balance
January 2004	307.9	238.6	69.3
February 2004	335.2	368.7	-33.6
March 2004	382.0	403.6	-21.6
April 2004	362.1	356.7	5.4
May 2004	353.0	365.7	-12.7
June 2004	364.9	389.9	-25.0
July 2004	370.5	423.5	-52.9
August 2004	363.7	387.2	-23.5
September 2004	361.3	405.8	-44.6
October 2004	412.8	407.3	5.5
November 2004	367.8	397.7	-29.9
December 2004	377.2	382.4	-5.2
TOTAL 2004	4,358.3	4,527.1	-168.8

2006 : U.S. trade in goods with Dominican Republic

NOTE: All figures are in millions of U.S. dollars on a nominal basis, not seasonally adjusted unless otherwise specified. Details may not equal totals due to rounding.

Month	Exports	Imports	Balance
January 2006	381.7	273.8	107.9
February 2006	388.2	350.1	38.1
March 2006	469.1	428.2	40.9
April 2006	372.5	333.5	39.0
May 2006	434.5	396.5	38.0
June 2006	447.3	383.2	64.1
July 2006	434.3	391.4	42.9
August 2006	480.5	412.0	68.5
September 2006	491.0	400.3	90.7
October 2006	510.6	430.0	80.5
November 2006	502.8	367.2	135.6
December 2006	438.1	366.2	71.9
TOTAL 2006	5,350.5	4,532.4	818.2

2007 : U.S. trade in goods with Dominican Republic

NOTE: All figures are in millions of U.S. dollars on a nominal basis, not seasonally adjusted unless otherwise specified. Details may not equal totals due to rounding.

Month	Exports	Imports	Balance
January 2007	419.3	242.8	176.5
February 2007	489.5	353.5	136.0
March 2007	497.6	396.0	101.7
April 2007	424.3	348.8	75.5
May 2007	477.7	381.2	96.5
June 2007	487.0	346.8	140.2
July 2007	499.9	362.8	137.0
August 2007	564.3	390.9	173.4
September 2007	436.5	350.8	85.8
October 2007	588.0	371.8	216.3
November 2007	602.6	358.3	244.4
December 2007	597.3	312.0	285.3
TOTAL 2007	**6,084.1**	**4,215.6**	**1,868.4**

2008 : U.S. trade in goods with Dominican Republic

NOTE: All figures are in millions of U.S. dollars on a nominal basis, not seasonally adjusted unless otherwise specified. Details may not equal totals due to rounding.

Month	Exports	Imports	Balance
January 2008	516.9	246.7	270.1
February 2008	519.7	346.5	173.3
March 2008	582.5	334.0	248.5
April 2008	658.3	390.3	268.0
May 2008	528.8	313.4	215.4
June 2008	483.6	341.8	141.8
July 2008	645.2	379.0	266.2
August 2008	666.4	325.5	340.9
September 2008	468.2	321.7	146.5
October 2008	566.1	363.5	202.6
November 2008	521.7	307.5	214.2
December 2008	437.1	308.0	129.0
TOTAL 2008	6,594.4	3,977.8	2,616.5

2009 : U.S. trade in goods with Dominican Republic

NOTE: All figures are in millions of U.S. dollars on a nominal basis, not seasonally adjusted unless otherwise specified. Details may not equal totals due to rounding.

Month	Exports	Imports	Balance
January 2009	450.6	186.0	264.6
February 2009	375.5	275.2	100.3
March 2009	436.2	313.9	122.3
April 2009	422.0	281.8	140.1
May 2009	411.8	264.3	147.6
June 2009	443.4	297.7	145.7
July 2009	464.6	292.3	172.3
August 2009	408.4	277.4	131.0
September 2009	419.5	303.3	116.2
October 2009	483.1	282.9	200.2
November 2009	477.2	280.1	197.1
December 2009	476.4	274.4	202.0
TOTAL 2009	**5,268.8**	**3,329.5**	**1,939.4**

2010 : U.S. trade in goods with Dominican Republic

NOTE: All figures are in millions of U.S. dollars on a nominal basis, not seasonally adjusted unless otherwise specified. Details may not equal totals due to rounding.

Month	Exports	Imports	Balance
January 2010	467.2	183.3	283.9
February 2010	501.8	269.2	232.6
March 2010	565.7	354.9	210.8
April 2010	562.7	312.3	250.4
May 2010	566.3	295.2	271.1
June 2010	545.3	351.9	193.4
July 2010	529.1	318.2	210.9
August 2010	480.5	330.1	150.4
September 2010	569.0	317.6	251.4
October 2010	589.4	327.1	262.3
November 2010	601.2	316.2	285.0
December 2010	601.1	295.6	305.5
TOTAL 2010	6,579.3	3,671.7	2,907.6

2000 : U.S. trade in goods with El Salvador

NOTE: All figures are in millions of U.S. dollars on a nominal basis, not seasonally adjusted unless otherwise specified. Details may not equal totals due to rounding.

Month	Exports	Imports	Balance
January 2000	117.1	124.1	-7.0
February 2000	124.2	161.9	-37.7
March 2000	163.2	181.6	-18.4
April 2000	133.4	133.8	-0.4
May 2000	143.8	166.7	-22.9
June 2000	161.8	171.3	-9.5
July 2000	141.7	172.4	-30.7
August 2000	174.2	178.5	-4.3
September 2000	158.6	156.3	2.3
October 2000	165.3	182.9	-17.6
November 2000	152.8	154.3	-1.5
December 2000	144.1	149.2	-5.1
TOTAL 2000	**1,780.2**	**1,933.0**	**-152.8**

2001 : U.S. trade in goods with El Salvador

NOTE: All figures are in millions of U.S. dollars on a nominal basis, not seasonally adjusted unless otherwise specified. Details may not equal totals due to rounding.

Month	Exports	Imports	Balance
January 2001	140.1	121.4	18.7
February 2001	146.1	148.9	-2.8
March 2001	161.2	180.9	-19.7
April 2001	150.6	138.9	11.7
May 2001	144.3	153.0	-8.7
June 2001	140.8	160.4	-19.6
July 2001	127.5	171.0	-43.5
August 2001	141.8	164.9	-23.1
September 2001	139.7	163.5	-23.8
October 2001	145.0	171.3	-26.3
November 2001	151.8	145.9	5.9
December 2001	170.5	160.2	10.3
TOTAL 2001	1,759.4	1,880.3	-120.9

2002 : U.S. trade in goods with El Salvador

NOTE: All figures are in millions of U.S. dollars on a nominal basis, not seasonally adjusted unless otherwise specified. Details may not equal totals due to rounding.

Month	Exports	Imports	Balance
January 2002	121.0	146.1	-25.1
February 2002	120.6	143.3	-22.7
March 2002	144.8	156.6	-11.8
April 2002	130.8	132.0	-1.2
May 2002	143.3	206.8	-63.5
June 2002	145.2	155.5	-10.3
July 2002	133.3	187.5	-54.2
August 2002	145.1	167.4	-22.3
September 2002	134.9	177.4	-42.5
October 2002	151.7	186.9	-35.2
November 2002	155.2	151.4	3.8
December 2002	138.2	171.4	-33.2
TOTAL 2002	1,664.1	1,982.3	-318.2

2003 : U.S. trade in goods with El Salvador

NOTE: All figures are in millions of U.S. dollars on a nominal basis, not seasonally adjusted unless otherwise specified. Details may not equal totals due to rounding.

Month	Exports	Imports	Balance
January 2003	138.4	148.4	-10.0
February 2003	152.4	153.4	-0.9
March 2003	182.9	189.0	-6.2
April 2003	161.5	159.6	1.9
May 2003	165.1	162.5	2.6
June 2003	137.3	154.2	-16.9
July 2003	134.4	187.6	-53.2
August 2003	159.1	165.0	-5.8
September 2003	141.8	184.3	-42.5
October 2003	139.6	186.5	-46.8
November 2003	169.4	144.1	25.2
December 2003	139.0	185.2	-46.2
TOTAL 2003	**1,820.9**	**2,019.8**	**-198.9**

2004 : U.S. trade in goods with El Salvador

NOTE: All figures are in millions of U.S. dollars on a nominal basis, not seasonally adjusted unless otherwise specified. Details may not equal totals due to rounding.

Month	Exports	Imports	Balance
January 2004	134.9	138.9	-4.0
February 2004	158.6	155.8	2.8
March 2004	172.7	179.6	-6.9
April 2004	177.7	149.6	28.1
May 2004	184.0	155.2	28.7
June 2004	165.7	187.3	-21.6
July 2004	144.3	205.7	-61.5
August 2004	146.9	170.3	-23.4
September 2004	132.2	186.2	-54.1
October 2004	163.6	173.2	-9.6
November 2004	146.8	174.7	-27.9
December 2004	140.4	175.6	-35.2
TOTAL 2004	**1,867.7**	**2,052.2**	**-184.5**

2006 : U.S. trade in goods with El Salvador

NOTE: All figures are in millions of U.S. dollars on a nominal basis, not seasonally adjusted unless otherwise specified. Details may not equal totals due to rounding.

Month	Exports	Imports	Balance
January 2006	164.6	122.1	42.5
February 2006	148.8	158.1	-9.2
March 2006	176.6	93.0	83.6
April 2006	175.8	106.9	68.9
May 2006	214.5	157.7	56.8
June 2006	181.8	172.9	8.9
July 2006	174.1	187.8	-13.7
August 2006	165.6	191.6	-26.0
September 2006	166.1	178.9	-12.9
October 2006	229.0	169.3	59.8
November 2006	178.1	160.1	17.9
December 2006	177.0	158.3	18.7
TOTAL 2006	2,152.1	1,856.8	295.3

2007 : U.S. trade in goods with El Salvador

NOTE: All figures are in millions of U.S. dollars on a nominal basis, not seasonally adjusted unless otherwise specified. Details may not equal totals due to rounding.

Month	Exports	Imports	Balance
January 2007	163.4	153.4	9.9
February 2007	167.5	154.2	13.3
March 2007	202.6	168.3	34.4
April 2007	201.3	144.7	56.6
May 2007	179.4	160.5	18.9
June 2007	193.3	173.8	19.4
July 2007	217.8	192.7	25.2
August 2007	206.4	205.6	0.8
September 2007	175.3	192.3	-17.0
October 2007	211.4	191.6	19.8
November 2007	194.7	155.0	39.8
December 2007	200.0	151.6	48.4
TOTAL 2007	**2,313.1**	**2,043.5**	**269.6**

2008 : U.S. trade in goods with El Salvador

NOTE: All figures are in millions of U.S. dollars on a nominal basis, not seasonally adjusted unless otherwise specified. Details may not equal totals due to rounding.

Month	Exports	Imports	Balance
January 2008	197.2	144.2	52.9
February 2008	214.7	174.0	40.7
March 2008	209.3	180.5	28.8
April 2008	218.8	181.1	37.7
May 2008	212.2	185.9	26.4
June 2008	212.2	212.8	-0.7
July 2008	245.5	239.9	5.7
August 2008	231.3	184.1	47.2
September 2008	187.0	200.3	-13.3
October 2008	189.3	188.2	1.1
November 2008	180.2	166.1	14.2
December 2008	164.2	170.9	-6.7
TOTAL 2008	2,462.0	2,228.0	234.0

2009 : U.S. trade in goods with El Salvador

NOTE: All figures are in millions of U.S. dollars on a nominal basis, not seasonally adjusted unless otherwise specified. Details may not equal totals due to rounding.

Month	Exports	Imports	Balance
January 2009	169.7	131.0	38.7
February 2009	167.8	141.0	26.8
March 2009	180.1	162.0	18.1
April 2009	160.8	121.7	39.1
May 2009	175.7	141.2	34.5
June 2009	160.3	163.0	-2.8
July 2009	168.8	181.8	-13.0
August 2009	162.1	156.3	5.9
September 2009	152.5	167.3	-14.7
October 2009	169.7	159.5	10.2
November 2009	171.0	145.1	25.9
December 2009	180.0	151.9	28.1
TOTAL 2009	2,018.7	1,821.8	196.9

2010 : U.S. trade in goods with El Salvador

NOTE: All figures are in millions of U.S. dollars on a nominal basis, not seasonally adjusted unless otherwise specified. Details may not equal totals due to rounding.

Month	Exports	Imports	Balance
January 2010	152.0	126.3	25.7
February 2010	191.0	150.7	40.3
March 2010	251.5	189.2	62.3
April 2010	228.7	152.3	76.5
May 2010	193.3	180.3	13.0
June 2010	212.4	196.9	15.5
July 2010	201.9	226.9	-25.0
August 2010	191.3	219.7	-28.4
September 2010	189.9	211.5	-21.7
October 2010	198.4	205.5	-7.1
November 2010	199.8	161.9	37.8
December 2010	223.1	184.5	38.5
TOTAL 2010	2,433.1	2,205.7	227.4

2000 : U.S. trade in goods with Guatemala

NOTE: All figures are in millions of U.S. dollars on a nominal basis, not seasonally adjusted unless otherwise specified. Details may not equal totals due to rounding.

Month	Exports	Imports	Balance
January 2000	137.8	197.4	-59.6
February 2000	138.5	217.8	-79.3
March 2000	167.8	231.9	-64.1
April 2000	148.9	193.3	-44.4
May 2000	147.0	211.5	-64.5
June 2000	150.1	247.5	-97.4
July 2000	158.2	235.7	-77.5
August 2000	151.0	241.3	-90.3
September 2000	160.9	214.6	-53.7
October 2000	172.1	214.9	-42.8
November 2000	185.6	192.3	-6.7
December 2000	182.8	209.3	-26.5
TOTAL 2000	1,900.7	2,607.5	-706.8

2001 : U.S. trade in goods with Guatemala

NOTE: All figures are in millions of U.S. dollars on a nominal basis, not seasonally adjusted unless otherwise specified. Details may not equal totals due to rounding.

Month	Exports	Imports	Balance
January 2001	156.6	228.7	-72.1
February 2001	159.5	202.8	-43.3
March 2001	169.9	255.6	-85.7
April 2001	165.4	209.3	-43.9
May 2001	147.5	229.0	-81.5
June 2001	148.7	228.6	-79.9
July 2001	134.3	239.8	-105.5
August 2001	150.2	234.5	-84.3
September 2001	140.8	180.2	-39.4
October 2001	163.3	197.8	-34.5
November 2001	185.9	194.1	-8.2
December 2001	147.6	188.2	-40.6
TOTAL 2001	**1,869.7**	**2,588.6**	**-718.9**

2002 : U.S. trade in goods with Guatemala

NOTE: All figures are in millions of U.S. dollars on a nominal basis, not seasonally adjusted unless otherwise specified. Details may not equal totals due to rounding.

Month	Exports	Imports	Balance
January 2002	153.7	216.5	-62.8
February 2002	150.1	195.7	-45.6
March 2002	179.9	224.2	-44.3
April 2002	155.0	255.2	-100.2
May 2002	171.4	237.4	-66.0
June 2002	178.2	206.1	-27.9
July 2002	170.0	253.7	-83.7
August 2002	168.4	263.7	-95.3
September 2002	149.9	239.5	-89.6
October 2002	191.2	246.2	-55.0
November 2002	203.6	218.0	-14.4
December 2002	173.0	240.2	-67.2
TOTAL 2002	**2,044.4**	**2,796.4**	**-752.0**

2003 : U.S. trade in goods with Guatemala

NOTE: All figures are in millions of U.S. dollars on a nominal basis, not seasonally adjusted unless otherwise specified. Details may not equal totals due to rounding.

Month	Exports	Imports	Balance
January 2003	215.2	246.9	-31.7
February 2003	193.5	238.1	-44.7
March 2003	241.4	261.6	-20.2
April 2003	172.3	263.5	-91.2
May 2003	188.5	248.1	-59.5
June 2003	170.3	233.1	-62.9
July 2003	190.3	267.9	-77.7
August 2003	162.2	258.9	-96.7
September 2003	171.6	248.4	-76.8
October 2003	180.5	220.7	-40.2
November 2003	201.3	202.5	-1.2
December 2003	176.5	257.1	-80.6
TOTAL 2003	2,263.4	2,946.8	-683.4

2004 : U.S. trade in goods with Guatemala

NOTE: All figures are in millions of U.S. dollars on a nominal basis, not seasonally adjusted unless otherwise specified. Details may not equal totals due to rounding.

Month	Exports	Imports	Balance
January 2004	172.2	217.0	-44.8
February 2004	192.1	223.6	-31.5
March 2004	218.0	308.6	-90.6
April 2004	205.9	255.5	-49.6
May 2004	202.7	242.8	-40.1
June 2004	184.8	286.9	-102.1
July 2004	214.3	299.6	-85.3
August 2004	213.2	275.7	-62.4
September 2004	186.4	254.4	-67.9
October 2004	236.2	251.1	-14.9
November 2004	255.9	259.0	-3.1
December 2004	269.6	279.8	-10.2
TOTAL 2004	**2,551.3**	**3,154.0**	**-602.7**

2006 : U.S. trade in goods with Guatemala

NOTE: All figures are in millions of U.S. dollars on a nominal basis, not seasonally adjusted unless otherwise specified. Details may not equal totals due to rounding.

Month	Exports	Imports	Balance
January 2006	253.9	215.1	38.8
February 2006	283.0	228.3	54.7
March 2006	308.6	321.5	-13.0
April 2006	288.6	235.5	53.1
May 2006	266.4	290.4	-24.0
June 2006	326.0	283.4	42.6
July 2006	307.0	272.2	34.8
August 2006	300.2	264.6	35.7
September 2006	272.7	269.3	3.4
October 2006	311.8	246.0	65.8
November 2006	312.0	244.6	67.4
December 2006	281.2	231.4	49.8
TOTAL 2006	3,511.4	3,102.3	409.1

2007 : U.S. trade in goods with Guatemala

NOTE: All figures are in millions of U.S. dollars on a nominal basis, not seasonally adjusted unless otherwise specified. Details may not equal totals due to rounding.

Month	Exports	Imports	Balance
January 2007	336.3	230.1	106.2
February 2007	268.6	239.8	28.8
March 2007	332.0	285.1	46.9
April 2007	315.1	297.7	17.4
May 2007	353.6	278.4	75.2
June 2007	328.9	250.3	78.6
July 2007	321.7	272.6	49.1
August 2007	345.6	265.2	80.4
September 2007	283.7	235.3	48.3
October 2007	424.1	247.1	177.0
November 2007	344.4	214.9	129.6
December 2007	411.1	209.8	201.3
TOTAL 2007	4,065.1	3,026.1	1,039.0

2008 : U.S. trade in goods with Guatemala

NOTE: All figures are in millions of U.S. dollars on a nominal basis, not seasonally adjusted unless otherwise specified. Details may not equal totals due to rounding.

Month	Exports	Imports	Balance
January 2008	339.3	297.7	41.6
February 2008	357.4	279.4	77.9
March 2008	383.9	291.5	92.4
April 2008	471.8	343.8	128.1
May 2008	367.0	313.1	53.9
June 2008	478.9	269.7	209.2
July 2008	439.9	374.1	65.8
August 2008	385.7	280.3	105.4
September 2008	416.6	280.2	136.3
October 2008	439.3	296.5	142.9
November 2008	326.9	188.8	138.1
December 2008	311.6	247.6	64.0
TOTAL 2008	4,718.3	3,462.7	1,255.5

2009 : U.S. trade in goods with Guatemala

NOTE: All figures are in millions of U.S. dollars on a nominal basis, not seasonally adjusted unless otherwise specified. Details may not equal totals due to rounding.

Month	Exports	Imports	Balance
January 2009	242.9	196.6	46.3
February 2009	365.0	203.0	161.9
March 2009	361.7	286.3	75.5
April 2009	272.6	272.4	0.2
May 2009	296.9	285.6	11.3
June 2009	324.6	263.5	61.1
July 2009	311.9	287.3	24.6
August 2009	333.7	285.1	48.5
September 2009	327.0	250.5	76.5
October 2009	332.7	276.8	55.8
November 2009	377.8	242.5	135.3
December 2009	327.8	298.0	29.8
TOTAL 2009	3,874.5	3,147.5	727.0

2010 : U.S. trade in goods with Guatemala

NOTE: All figures are in millions of U.S. dollars on a nominal basis, not seasonally adjusted unless otherwise specified. Details may not equal totals due to rounding.

Month	Exports	Imports	Balance
January 2010	328.0	243.2	84.8
February 2010	339.9	269.4	70.4
March 2010	431.5	307.5	124.0
April 2010	385.7	353.0	32.7
May 2010	412.0	295.6	116.4
June 2010	316.3	257.6	58.7
July 2010	328.8	250.3	78.5
August 2010	378.4	290.5	87.8
September 2010	366.9	248.2	118.6
October 2010	384.4	243.4	141.0
November 2010	392.6	199.4	193.2
December 2010	413.9	234.7	179.2
TOTAL 2010	4,478.3	3,193.0	1,285.3

2000 : U.S. trade in goods with Honduras

NOTE: All figures are in millions of U.S. dollars on a nominal basis, not seasonally adjusted unless otherwise specified. Details may not equal totals due to rounding.

Month	Exports	Imports	Balance
January 2000	190.2	178.3	11.9
February 2000	209.8	256.1	-46.3
March 2000	233.3	286.8	-53.5
April 2000	210.8	233.5	-22.7
May 2000	211.2	256.3	-45.1
June 2000	219.2	273.3	-54.1
July 2000	200.3	270.2	-69.9
August 2000	249.2	277.1	-27.9
September 2000	212.7	240.1	-27.4
October 2000	220.8	275.9	-55.1
November 2000	222.7	287.5	-64.8
December 2000	203.8	255.0	-51.2
TOTAL 2000	**2,584.0**	**3,090.1**	**-506.1**

2001 : U.S. trade in goods with Honduras

NOTE: All figures are in millions of U.S. dollars on a nominal basis, not seasonally adjusted unless otherwise specified. Details may not equal totals due to rounding.

Month	Exports	Imports	Balance
January 2001	205.6	206.7	-1.1
February 2001	206.3	266.4	-60.1
March 2001	238.3	300.9	-62.6
April 2001	197.0	248.8	-51.8
May 2001	206.7	280.7	-74.0
June 2001	207.4	261.8	-54.4
July 2001	179.6	280.5	-100.9
August 2001	209.6	261.3	-51.7
September 2001	200.4	239.3	-38.9
October 2001	195.3	267.8	-72.5
November 2001	181.0	266.9	-85.9
December 2001	188.6	245.4	-56.8
TOTAL 2001	2,415.8	3,126.5	-710.7

2002 : U.S. trade in goods with Honduras

NOTE: All figures are in millions of U.S. dollars on a nominal basis, not seasonally adjusted unless otherwise specified. Details may not equal totals due to rounding.

Month	Exports	Imports	Balance
January 2002	191.9	194.6	-2.7
February 2002	191.7	249.1	-57.4
March 2002	205.8	263.7	-57.9
April 2002	201.8	242.3	-40.5
May 2002	224.1	276.0	-51.9
June 2002	217.0	266.6	-49.6
July 2002	195.7	313.2	-117.5
August 2002	226.5	293.8	-67.3
September 2002	215.4	285.2	-69.8
October 2002	231.7	305.9	-74.2
November 2002	258.3	271.2	-12.9
December 2002	211.2	299.7	-88.5
TOTAL 2002	**2,571.1**	**3,261.3**	**-690.2**

2003 : U.S. trade in goods with Honduras

NOTE: All figures are in millions of U.S. dollars on a nominal basis, not seasonally adjusted unless otherwise specified. Details may not equal totals due to rounding.

Month	Exports	Imports	Balance
January 2003	228.9	215.3	13.6
February 2003	233.3	263.0	-29.7
March 2003	250.7	304.2	-53.6
April 2003	236.8	264.3	-27.5
May 2003	229.2	284.1	-54.9
June 2003	236.5	277.8	-41.3
July 2003	221.1	300.0	-79.0
August 2003	246.8	270.7	-24.0
September 2003	221.7	280.0	-58.3
October 2003	248.8	297.7	-48.9
November 2003	244.4	252.9	-8.5
December 2003	228.1	302.6	-74.4
TOTAL 2003	2,826.2	3,312.7	-486.4

2004 : U.S. trade in goods with Honduras

NOTE: All figures are in millions of U.S. dollars on a nominal basis, not seasonally adjusted unless otherwise specified. Details may not equal totals due to rounding.

Month	Exports	Imports	Balance
January 2004	228.8	211.7	17.1
February 2004	234.3	281.2	-46.9
March 2004	272.5	340.1	-67.6
April 2004	263.4	269.9	-6.5
May 2004	262.9	305.9	-43.0
June 2004	232.0	334.4	-102.4
July 2004	247.6	327.1	-79.5
August 2004	254.7	329.9	-75.2
September 2004	258.8	289.0	-30.2
October 2004	294.1	304.7	-10.6
November 2004	269.4	323.9	-54.5
December 2004	259.8	322.0	-62.3
TOTAL 2004	**3,078.4**	**3,640.0**	**-561.6**

2006 : U.S. trade in goods with Honduras

NOTE: All figures are in millions of U.S. dollars on a nominal basis, not seasonally adjusted unless otherwise specified. Details may not equal totals due to rounding.

Month	Exports	Imports	Balance
January 2006	283.6	256.0	27.6
February 2006	253.6	303.6	-50.0
March 2006	318.3	340.4	-22.1
April 2006	311.5	206.9	104.6
May 2006	335.8	319.5	16.2
June 2006	331.8	349.8	-18.0
July 2006	283.9	324.3	-40.4
August 2006	320.4	346.2	-25.8
September 2006	311.5	323.7	-12.2
October 2006	329.9	314.6	15.3
November 2006	296.0	334.6	-38.6
December 2006	310.7	297.8	12.9
TOTAL 2006	3,687.1	3,717.5	-30.4

2007 : U.S. trade in goods with Honduras

NOTE: All figures are in millions of U.S. dollars on a nominal basis, not seasonally adjusted unless otherwise specified. Details may not equal totals due to rounding.

Month	Exports	Imports	Balance
January 2007	313.0	254.4	58.6
February 2007	330.8	294.9	35.8
March 2007	354.8	347.6	7.2
April 2007	358.8	300.6	58.2
May 2007	393.0	359.3	33.7
June 2007	342.7	344.3	-1.6
July 2007	445.8	343.8	102.0
August 2007	367.5	369.8	-2.3
September 2007	361.6	312.3	49.3
October 2007	377.7	346.1	31.6
November 2007	377.8	333.7	44.1
December 2007	437.9	305.3	132.6
TOTAL 2007	4,461.4	3,912.1	549.3

2008 : U.S. trade in goods with Honduras

NOTE: All figures are in millions of U.S. dollars on a nominal basis, not seasonally adjusted unless otherwise specified. Details may not equal totals due to rounding.

Month	Exports	Imports	Balance
January 2008	418.0	249.7	168.3
February 2008	408.4	326.4	82.0
March 2008	399.7	328.4	71.3
April 2008	422.1	343.8	78.3
May 2008	405.7	336.0	69.7
June 2008	469.9	376.6	93.2
July 2008	473.4	378.3	95.1
August 2008	457.8	345.8	112.0
September 2008	385.5	359.1	26.4
October 2008	378.2	382.3	-4.1
November 2008	351.0	307.0	44.1
December 2008	276.6	307.9	-31.3
TOTAL 2008	4,846.2	4,041.2	805.0

2009 : U.S. trade in goods with Honduras

NOTE: All figures are in millions of U.S. dollars on a nominal basis, not seasonally adjusted unless otherwise specified. Details may not equal totals due to rounding.

Month	Exports	Imports	Balance
January 2009	239.8	201.3	38.5
February 2009	271.8	257.9	13.9
March 2009	291.9	296.9	-5.1
April 2009	257.7	228.0	29.7
May 2009	283.0	275.2	7.8
June 2009	270.4	286.9	-16.5
July 2009	294.2	296.5	-2.3
August 2009	267.5	293.6	-26.0
September 2009	247.1	287.5	-40.4
October 2009	301.9	295.3	6.6
November 2009	324.6	305.7	18.8
December 2009	317.7	294.5	23.1
TOTAL 2009	**3,367.6**	**3,319.3**	**48.3**

2010 : U.S. trade in goods with Honduras

NOTE: All figures are in millions of U.S. dollars on a nominal basis, not seasonally adjusted unless otherwise specified. Details may not equal totals due to rounding.

Month	Exports	Imports	Balance
January 2010	323.1	221.3	101.8
February 2010	340.9	288.3	52.6
March 2010	397.4	352.5	44.9
April 2010	377.3	268.2	109.2
May 2010	410.4	336.9	73.5
June 2010	379.3	366.9	12.4
July 2010	374.8	345.7	29.1
August 2010	397.4	352.1	45.2
September 2010	373.8	354.1	19.7
October 2010	451.3	348.0	103.3
November 2010	389.3	347.9	41.4
December 2010	391.3	350.4	40.9
TOTAL 2010	4,606.4	3,932.3	674.1

2000 : U.S. trade in goods with Nicaragua

NOTE: All figures are in millions of U.S. dollars on a nominal basis, not seasonally adjusted unless otherwise specified. Details may not equal totals due to rounding.

Month	Exports	Imports	Balance
January 2000	29.4	39.0	-9.6
February 2000	32.0	50.4	-18.4
March 2000	36.0	59.1	-23.1
April 2000	29.9	42.1	-12.2
May 2000	31.9	44.5	-12.6
June 2000	28.0	56.4	-28.4
July 2000	34.3	58.5	-24.2
August 2000	27.8	47.7	-19.9
September 2000	32.4	44.9	-12.5
October 2000	38.6	47.1	-8.5
November 2000	28.7	53.7	-25.0
December 2000	31.1	45.0	-13.9
TOTAL 2000	380.1	588.4	-208.3

2001 : U.S. trade in goods with Nicaragua

NOTE: All figures are in millions of U.S. dollars on a nominal basis, not seasonally adjusted unless otherwise specified. Details may not equal totals due to rounding.

Month	Exports	Imports	Balance
January 2001	41.5	51.9	-10.4
February 2001	32.9	49.6	-16.7
March 2001	42.8	57.9	-15.1
April 2001	43.0	42.5	0.5
May 2001	34.1	54.2	-20.1
June 2001	41.0	50.3	-9.3
July 2001	32.3	55.5	-23.2
August 2001	45.1	61.1	-16.0
September 2001	29.4	51.5	-22.1
October 2001	33.7	49.9	-16.2
November 2001	30.8	41.7	-10.9
December 2001	36.4	37.7	-1.3
TOTAL 2001	443.0	603.8	-160.8

2002 : U.S. trade in goods with Nicaragua

NOTE: All figures are in millions of U.S. dollars on a nominal basis, not seasonally adjusted unless otherwise specified. Details may not equal totals due to rounding.

Month	Exports	Imports	Balance
January 2002	24.0	49.8	-25.8
February 2002	38.2	53.7	-15.5
March 2002	37.8	67.0	-29.2
April 2002	30.9	51.1	-20.2
May 2002	35.5	52.5	-17.0
June 2002	38.4	49.0	-10.6
July 2002	34.4	60.1	-25.7
August 2002	42.9	62.5	-19.6
September 2002	31.5	61.1	-29.6
October 2002	35.7	59.8	-24.1
November 2002	46.7	55.9	-9.2
December 2002	41.0	57.0	-16.0
TOTAL 2002	**437.0**	**679.5**	**-242.5**

2003 : U.S. trade in goods with Nicaragua

NOTE: All figures are in millions of U.S. dollars on a nominal basis, not seasonally adjusted unless otherwise specified. Details may not equal totals due to rounding.

Month	Exports	Imports	Balance
January 2003	36.7	60.3	-23.6
February 2003	40.3	57.0	-16.7
March 2003	48.3	73.1	-24.8
April 2003	42.9	65.4	-22.4
May 2003	36.0	57.8	-21.8
June 2003	33.1	59.2	-26.1
July 2003	41.3	68.2	-26.8
August 2003	39.6	66.2	-26.5
September 2003	42.1	62.8	-20.6
October 2003	54.5	67.3	-12.8
November 2003	50.2	59.9	-9.7
December 2003	36.7	72.8	-36.2
TOTAL 2003	501.7	769.7	-268.1

2004 : U.S. trade in goods with Nicaragua

NOTE: All figures are in millions of U.S. dollars on a nominal basis, not seasonally adjusted unless otherwise specified. Details may not equal totals due to rounding.

Month	Exports	Imports	Balance
January 2004	36.5	61.8	-25.3
February 2004	40.6	75.9	-35.2
March 2004	61.1	85.1	-24.0
April 2004	47.8	68.0	-20.2
May 2004	56.7	67.3	-10.7
June 2004	52.2	85.7	-33.6
July 2004	42.4	85.3	-42.9
August 2004	54.8	103.5	-48.6
September 2004	47.4	90.3	-42.9
October 2004	45.3	91.2	-45.9
November 2004	50.4	91.7	-41.3
December 2004	57.3	84.6	-27.3
TOTAL 2004	**592.4**	**990.3**	**-397.9**

2006 : U.S. trade in goods with Nicaragua

NOTE: All figures are in millions of U.S. dollars on a nominal basis, not seasonally adjusted unless otherwise specified. Details may not equal totals due to rounding.

Month	Exports	Imports	Balance
January 2006	53.8	109.8	-56.1
February 2006	54.7	149.1	-94.4
March 2006	69.5	125.0	-55.5
April 2006	64.1	115.9	-51.8
May 2006	74.0	114.0	-40.0
June 2006	59.8	147.2	-87.4
July 2006	61.9	119.6	-57.7
August 2006	54.1	136.4	-82.3
September 2006	57.0	120.1	-63.1
October 2006	70.3	149.2	-79.0
November 2006	79.2	120.3	-41.1
December 2006	53.2	119.1	-65.9
TOTAL 2006	751.6	1,526.0	-774.4

2007 : U.S. trade in goods with Nicaragua

NOTE: All figures are in millions of U.S. dollars on a nominal basis, not seasonally adjusted unless otherwise specified. Details may not equal totals due to rounding.

Month	Exports	Imports	Balance
January 2007	61.1	117.4	-56.4
February 2007	54.4	113.5	-59.2
March 2007	73.1	121.8	-48.7
April 2007	70.2	126.5	-56.3
May 2007	69.7	130.8	-61.1
June 2007	68.7	123.2	-54.5
July 2007	72.2	145.6	-73.4
August 2007	86.7	155.2	-68.5
September 2007	117.5	126.2	-8.7
October 2007	62.0	155.5	-93.5
November 2007	76.7	145.0	-68.3
December 2007	77.7	142.7	-65.0
TOTAL 2007	**890.0**	**1,603.5**	**-713.5**

2008 : U.S. trade in goods with Nicaragua

NOTE: All figures are in millions of U.S. dollars on a nominal basis, not seasonally adjusted unless otherwise specified. Details may not equal totals due to rounding.

Month	Exports	Imports	Balance
January 2008	70.9	128.2	-57.4
February 2008	60.1	150.0	-89.9
March 2008	89.3	136.6	-47.2
April 2008	76.2	148.7	-72.5
May 2008	78.5	127.2	-48.7
June 2008	116.0	146.6	-30.6
July 2008	97.7	162.0	-64.3
August 2008	90.6	159.1	-68.5
September 2008	79.3	160.3	-80.9
October 2008	135.4	141.0	-5.6
November 2008	117.4	121.7	-4.3
December 2008	82.7	122.2	-39.4
TOTAL 2008	1,094.2	1,703.6	-609.3

2009 : U.S. trade in goods with Nicaragua

NOTE: All figures are in millions of U.S. dollars on a nominal basis, not seasonally adjusted unless otherwise specified. Details may not equal totals due to rounding.

Month	Exports	Imports	Balance
January 2009	38.8	97.2	-58.4
February 2009	61.8	124.6	-62.8
March 2009	59.3	132.5	-73.2
April 2009	45.9	128.0	-82.0
May 2009	64.8	129.0	-64.2
June 2009	61.3	129.1	-67.8
July 2009	52.5	144.7	-92.2
August 2009	66.7	143.2	-76.5
September 2009	59.2	160.2	-101.0
October 2009	69.2	164.0	-94.8
November 2009	64.7	128.9	-64.2
December 2009	70.7	130.9	-60.2
TOTAL 2009	715.1	1,612.4	-897.3

2010 : U.S. trade in goods with Nicaragua

NOTE: All figures are in millions of U.S. dollars on a nominal basis, not seasonally adjusted unless otherwise specified. Details may not equal totals due to rounding.

Month	Exports	Imports	Balance
January 2010	45.3	112.0	-66.7
February 2010	71.8	149.5	-77.6
March 2010	72.7	175.2	-102.6
April 2010	104.1	164.8	-60.6
May 2010	79.0	160.1	-81.0
June 2010	82.8	171.6	-88.9
July 2010	64.7	195.4	-130.7
August 2010	85.0	178.9	-94.0
September 2010	83.8	172.6	-88.8
October 2010	127.4	191.5	-64.0
November 2010	66.8	166.3	-99.5
December 2010	97.9	169.6	-71.7
TOTAL 2010	981.3	2,007.5	-1,026.2

2006 : U.S. trade in goods with Korea, South

NOTE: All figures are in millions of U.S. dollars on a nominal basis, not seasonally adjusted unless otherwise specified. Details may not equal totals due to rounding.

Month	Exports	Imports	Balance
January 2006	2,506.0	3,890.9	-1,384.9
February 2006	2,344.4	3,559.6	-1,215.2
March 2006	2,976.8	3,773.1	-796.3
April 2006	2,729.2	3,561.1	-831.9
May 2006	2,411.5	4,061.5	-1,650.0
June 2006	2,725.5	3,885.6	-1,160.0
July 2006	2,555.7	3,854.0	-1,298.3
August 2006	2,888.3	4,015.6	-1,127.3
September 2006	2,878.2	3,687.5	-809.3
October 2006	2,632.3	3,965.0	-1,332.7
November 2006	2,615.6	3,836.7	-1,221.1
December 2006	2,955.6	3,713.0	-757.4
TOTAL 2006	**32,219.1**	**45,803.6**	**-13,584.5**

2007 : U.S. trade in goods with Korea, South

NOTE: All figures are in millions of U.S. dollars on a nominal basis, not seasonally adjusted unless otherwise specified. Details may not equal totals due to rounding.

Month	Exports	Imports	Balance
January 2007	2,691.2	4,220.1	-1,528.9
February 2007	2,540.9	3,600.5	-1,059.6
March 2007	2,954.6	4,211.7	-1,257.1
April 2007	2,989.8	4,047.0	-1,057.1
May 2007	2,733.5	4,273.2	-1,539.7
June 2007	3,062.6	3,997.2	-934.6
July 2007	2,788.8	4,259.6	-1,470.8
August 2007	2,910.2	3,792.0	-881.8
September 2007	2,581.7	3,517.3	-935.6
October 2007	3,188.7	3,937.0	-748.3
November 2007	2,902.2	4,215.4	-1,313.2
December 2007	3,057.4	3,491.3	-433.9
TOTAL 2007	34,401.7	47,562.3	-13,160.6

2008 : U.S. trade in goods with Korea, South

NOTE: All figures are in millions of U.S. dollars on a nominal basis, not seasonally adjusted unless otherwise specified. Details may not equal totals due to rounding.

Month	Exports	Imports	Balance
January 2008	2,738.7	3,890.4	-1,151.7
February 2008	2,745.6	3,828.4	-1,082.8
March 2008	3,191.9	4,006.2	-814.3
April 2008	3,145.2	4,403.5	-1,258.2
May 2008	3,091.5	4,261.9	-1,170.5
June 2008	3,387.4	3,960.8	-573.4
July 2008	3,197.3	4,500.0	-1,302.7
August 2008	3,092.8	3,859.0	-766.2
September 2008	2,931.7	4,130.7	-1,199.0
October 2008	2,911.5	4,326.0	-1,414.5
November 2008	2,373.8	3,617.0	-1,243.2
December 2008	1,861.3	3,285.2	-1,423.9
TOTAL 2008	**34,668.7**	**48,069.1**	**-13,400.4**

2009 : U.S. trade in goods with Korea, South

NOTE: All figures are in millions of U.S. dollars on a nominal basis, not seasonally adjusted unless otherwise specified. Details may not equal totals due to rounding.

Month	Exports	Imports	Balance
January 2009	1,669.6	3,600.0	-1,930.4
February 2009	1,975.4	2,864.0	-888.5
March 2009	2,030.6	3,185.3	-1,154.7
April 2009	2,055.4	3,090.8	-1,035.4
May 2009	2,466.5	3,191.8	-725.3
June 2009	2,375.8	3,287.4	-911.6
July 2009	2,392.3	3,393.9	-1,001.7
August 2009	2,696.0	3,121.1	-425.1
September 2009	2,611.7	3,368.1	-756.4
October 2009	2,898.1	3,426.5	-528.4
November 2009	2,626.6	3,312.6	-686.1
December 2009	2,814.0	3,374.2	-560.2
TOTAL 2009	28,611.9	39,215.6	-10,603.7

2010 : U.S. trade in goods with Korea, South

NOTE: All figures are in millions of U.S. dollars on a nominal basis, not seasonally adjusted unless otherwise specified. Details may not equal totals due to rounding.

Month	Exports	Imports	Balance
January 2010	2,716.8	3,102.9	-386.1
February 2010	2,969.5	3,113.1	-143.6
March 2010	3,738.8	3,725.6	13.3
April 2010	3,182.5	3,888.4	-706.0
May 2010	3,307.2	4,120.3	-813.0
June 2010	3,310.4	4,403.1	-1,092.7
July 2010	3,433.8	4,457.1	-1,023.3
August 2010	3,185.2	4,440.9	-1,255.6
September 2010	3,029.6	4,276.8	-1,247.1
October 2010	3,339.1	4,490.0	-1,150.9
November 2010	3,174.8	4,788.6	-1,613.8
December 2010	3,457.9	4,068.0	-610.1
TOTAL 2010	**38,845.7**	**48,874.6**	**-10,028.9**

2012 : U.S. trade in goods with Korea, South

NOTE: All figures are in millions of U.S. dollars on a nominal basis, not seasonally adjusted unless otherwise specified. Details may not equal totals due to rounding.

Month	Exports	Imports	Balance
January 2012	3,178.5	4,558.3	-1,379.8
February 2012	3,997.2	4,412.0	-414.7
March 2012	4,226.4	4,777.8	-551.4
April 2012	3,706.5	5,476.2	-1,769.7
May 2012	3,467.8	5,467.5	-1,999.6
June 2012	3,643.1	4,773.5	-1,130.4
July 2012	3,519.2	5,420.7	-1,901.6
August 2012	3,185.0	4,782.4	-1,597.4
September 2012	3,420.7	4,709.6	-1,288.9
October 2012	3,460.2	5,063.4	-1,603.3
November 2012	3,062.1	4,851.4	-1,789.3
December 2012	3,451.3	4,586.9	-1,135.6
TOTAL 2012	42,317.9	58,879.8	-16,561.8

1999 : U.S. trade in goods with Singapore

NOTE: All figures are in millions of U.S. dollars on a nominal basis, not seasonally adjusted unless otherwise specified. Details may not equal totals due to rounding.

Month	Exports	Imports	Balance
January 1999	1,475.3	1,397.2	78.1
February 1999	1,102.3	1,230.1	-127.8
March 1999	1,321.2	1,543.5	-222.3
April 1999	1,218.5	1,423.1	-204.6
May 1999	1,222.1	1,527.3	-305.2
June 1999	1,310.8	1,562.3	-251.5
July 1999	1,303.0	1,719.3	-416.3
August 1999	1,638.7	1,511.7	127.0
September 1999	1,494.5	1,517.4	-22.9
October 1999	1,372.2	1,597.7	-225.5
November 1999	1,279.8	1,589.5	-309.7
December 1999	1,508.9	1,572.2	-63.3
TOTAL 1999	16,247.3	18,191.3	-1,944.0

2000 : U.S. trade in goods with Singapore

NOTE: All figures are in millions of U.S. dollars on a nominal basis, not seasonally adjusted unless otherwise specified. Details may not equal totals due to rounding.

Month	Exports	Imports	Balance
January 2000	1,239.0	1,400.6	-161.6
February 2000	1,194.6	1,422.6	-228.0
March 2000	1,620.7	1,473.0	147.7
April 2000	1,324.9	1,386.2	-61.3
May 2000	1,273.9	1,516.6	-242.7
June 2000	1,499.4	1,625.4	-126.0
July 2000	1,504.0	1,647.4	-143.4
August 2000	1,669.5	1,837.1	-167.6
September 2000	1,754.3	1,785.4	-31.1
October 2000	1,662.2	1,704.7	-42.5
November 2000	1,515.6	1,787.8	-272.2
December 2000	1,548.2	1,591.5	-43.3
TOTAL 2000	**17,806.3**	**19,178.3**	**-1,372.0**

2001 : U.S. trade in goods with Singapore

NOTE: All figures are in millions of U.S. dollars on a nominal basis, not seasonally adjusted unless otherwise specified. Details may not equal totals due to rounding.

Month	Exports	Imports	Balance
January 2001	1,434.4	1,499.3	-64.9
February 2001	1,541.4	1,305.5	235.9
March 2001	1,689.1	1,372.6	316.5
April 2001	1,232.9	1,290.0	-57.1
May 2001	1,550.2	1,279.8	270.4
June 2001	1,452.7	1,186.8	265.9
July 2001	1,434.2	1,204.5	229.7
August 2001	1,370.0	1,203.4	166.6
September 2001	1,523.1	1,065.9	457.2
October 2001	1,765.8	1,289.1	476.7
November 2001	1,475.2	1,287.7	187.5
December 2001	1,182.8	1,015.4	167.4
TOTAL 2001	17,651.8	15,000.0	2,651.8

2002 : U.S. trade in goods with Singapore

NOTE: All figures are in millions of U.S. dollars on a nominal basis, not seasonally adjusted unless otherwise specified. Details may not equal totals due to rounding.

Month	Exports	Imports	Balance
January 2002	1,385.8	1,198.7	187.1
February 2002	1,069.1	1,050.3	18.8
March 2002	1,704.8	1,179.3	525.5
April 2002	1,329.1	1,208.6	120.5
May 2002	1,234.8	1,300.1	-65.3
June 2002	1,538.2	1,022.2	516.0
July 2002	1,322.5	1,244.8	77.7
August 2002	1,600.4	1,375.4	225.0
September 2002	1,133.0	1,232.3	-99.3
October 2002	1,582.9	1,333.9	249.0
November 2002	1,302.4	1,355.5	-53.1
December 2002	1,014.8	1,301.2	-286.4
TOTAL 2002	16,217.8	14,802.3	1,415.5

2003 : U.S. trade in goods with Singapore

NOTE: All figures are in millions of U.S. dollars on a nominal basis, not seasonally adjusted unless otherwise specified. Details may not equal totals due to rounding.

Month	Exports	Imports	Balance
January 2003	1,069.2	1,420.8	-351.7
February 2003	1,425.4	1,106.2	319.2
March 2003	1,565.6	1,231.3	334.3
April 2003	1,146.1	1,333.1	-187.0
May 2003	1,312.0	1,285.0	27.0
June 2003	1,340.5	1,365.4	-24.8
July 2003	1,598.6	1,238.7	359.9
August 2003	1,846.6	1,065.2	781.4
September 2003	1,258.4	1,345.5	-87.1
October 2003	1,449.6	1,341.6	108.0
November 2003	1,262.2	1,124.3	137.9
December 2003	1,285.9	1,280.6	5.3
TOTAL 2003	16,560.2	15,137.7	1,422.4

2005 : U.S. trade in goods with Singapore

NOTE: All figures are in millions of U.S. dollars on a nominal basis, not seasonally adjusted unless otherwise specified. Details may not equal totals due to rounding.

Month	Exports	Imports	Balance
January 2005	1,558.8	1,236.7	322.1
February 2005	1,563.7	1,136.0	427.7
March 2005	2,017.2	1,163.8	853.4
April 2005	1,610.3	1,268.9	341.4
May 2005	1,722.2	1,230.8	491.4
June 2005	1,696.3	1,254.1	442.2
July 2005	1,587.7	1,188.8	398.9
August 2005	1,743.5	1,338.2	405.3
September 2005	1,715.0	1,259.1	455.9
October 2005	1,933.4	1,312.7	620.7
November 2005	1,605.2	1,321.9	283.3
December 2005	1,712.7	1,399.0	313.7
TOTAL 2005	20,466.1	15,110.1	5,356.0

2006 : U.S. trade in goods with Singapore

NOTE: All figures are in millions of U.S. dollars on a nominal basis, not seasonally adjusted unless otherwise specified. Details may not equal totals due to rounding.

Month	Exports	Imports	Balance
January 2006	1,623.8	1,307.3	316.5
February 2006	1,697.4	1,239.0	458.4
March 2006	2,021.2	1,511.3	509.9
April 2006	2,007.6	1,471.0	536.6
May 2006	1,979.5	1,392.7	586.9
June 2006	1,815.2	1,545.5	269.6
July 2006	1,783.8	1,678.8	105.0
August 2006	2,082.5	1,665.4	417.0
September 2006	2,105.6	1,423.2	682.4
October 2006	1,984.7	1,643.9	340.7
November 2006	2,193.8	1,494.8	699.0
December 2006	2,530.6	1,395.2	1,135.4
TOTAL 2006	**23,825.5**	**17,768.1**	**6,057.5**

2007 : U.S. trade in goods with Singapore

NOTE: All figures are in millions of U.S. dollars on a nominal basis, not seasonally adjusted unless otherwise specified. Details may not equal totals due to rounding.

Month	Exports	Imports	Balance
January 2007	2,023.0	1,571.8	451.2
February 2007	2,068.3	1,413.1	655.2
March 2007	2,320.2	1,668.4	651.8
April 2007	1,910.6	1,518.6	392.0
May 2007	1,979.0	1,747.7	231.2
June 2007	2,275.2	1,451.6	823.6
July 2007	2,022.1	1,536.5	485.6
August 2007	2,175.1	1,535.1	640.0
September 2007	2,155.3	1,463.0	692.3
October 2007	2,122.5	1,568.8	553.7
November 2007	2,172.3	1,565.4	606.9
December 2007	2,395.0	1,353.6	1,041.4
TOTAL 2007	25,618.6	18,393.7	7,224.9

2008 : U.S. trade in goods with Singapore

NOTE: All figures are in millions of U.S. dollars on a nominal basis, not seasonally adjusted unless otherwise specified. Details may not equal totals due to rounding.

Month	Exports	Imports	Balance
January 2008	2,154.0	1,674.9	479.1
February 2008	2,396.1	1,385.0	1,011.1
March 2008	2,654.6	1,433.4	1,221.1
April 2008	2,492.1	1,396.5	1,095.6
May 2008	2,513.1	1,358.2	1,154.9
June 2008	2,596.1	1,208.1	1,388.0
July 2008	2,321.7	1,394.4	927.3
August 2008	2,444.3	1,202.9	1,241.4
September 2008	2,247.3	1,317.8	929.5
October 2008	2,283.3	1,240.1	1,043.2
November 2008	1,858.3	1,128.6	729.7
December 2008	1,892.9	1,145.1	747.8
TOTAL 2008	**27,853.6**	**15,884.9**	**11,968.7**

2009 : U.S. trade in goods with Singapore

NOTE: All figures are in millions of U.S. dollars on a nominal basis, not seasonally adjusted unless otherwise specified. Details may not equal totals due to rounding.

Month	Exports	Imports	Balance
January 2009	1,784.8	1,154.7	630.1
February 2009	1,593.4	881.2	712.2
March 2009	1,741.1	1,321.4	419.7
April 2009	1,570.1	1,228.0	342.1
May 2009	1,471.8	1,176.6	295.2
June 2009	1,791.6	1,268.4	523.2
July 2009	2,120.5	1,423.4	697.1
August 2009	1,849.6	1,572.1	277.5
September 2009	1,991.5	1,653.7	337.9
October 2009	2,294.5	1,479.2	815.3
November 2009	1,898.1	1,200.9	697.3
December 2009	2,124.9	1,345.5	779.4
TOTAL 2009	22,231.8	15,704.9	6,526.9

2001 : U.S. trade in goods with Oman

NOTE: All figures are in millions of U.S. dollars on a nominal basis, not seasonally adjusted unless otherwise specified. Details may not equal totals due to rounding.

Month	Exports	Imports	Balance
January 2001	16.4	26.3	-9.9
February 2001	21.8	35.1	-13.3
March 2001	19.2	22.6	-3.4
April 2001	22.9	26.4	-3.5
May 2001	18.6	17.4	1.2
June 2001	16.7	50.2	-33.5
July 2001	18.3	81.6	-63.3
August 2001	19.1	97.5	-78.4
September 2001	25.9	17.3	8.6
October 2001	25.2	11.8	13.4
November 2001	20.0	19.0	1.0
December 2001	82.2	14.9	67.3
TOTAL 2001	306.3	420.1	-113.8

2002 : U.S. trade in goods with Oman

NOTE: All figures are in millions of U.S. dollars on a nominal basis, not seasonally adjusted unless otherwise specified. Details may not equal totals due to rounding.

Month	Exports	Imports	Balance
January 2002	61.6	33.2	28.4
February 2002	12.9	42.0	-29.1
March 2002	21.0	29.4	-8.4
April 2002	16.4	31.2	-14.8
May 2002	64.0	14.1	49.9
June 2002	66.7	12.4	54.3
July 2002	15.8	52.8	-37.0
August 2002	18.8	43.3	-24.5
September 2002	20.6	70.7	-50.1
October 2002	23.4	17.8	5.6
November 2002	16.2	33.6	-17.4
December 2002	18.6	20.0	-1.4
TOTAL 2002	356.0	400.5	-44.5

2003 : U.S. trade in goods with Oman

NOTE: All figures are in millions of U.S. dollars on a nominal basis, not seasonally adjusted unless otherwise specified. Details may not equal totals due to rounding.

Month	Exports	Imports	Balance
January 2003	18.9	66.5	-47.6
February 2003	14.5	64.6	-50.2
March 2003	28.0	19.8	8.2
April 2003	24.5	52.0	-27.5
May 2003	19.7	65.1	-45.4
June 2003	21.8	30.8	-9.0
July 2003	82.6	18.3	64.2
August 2003	15.3	117.4	-102.1
September 2003	20.3	89.2	-69.0
October 2003	21.4	61.3	-39.9
November 2003	26.3	93.6	-67.2
December 2003	29.2	16.1	13.2
TOTAL 2003	**322.4**	**694.7**	**-372.3**

2004 : U.S. trade in goods with Oman

NOTE: All figures are in millions of U.S. dollars on a nominal basis, not seasonally adjusted unless otherwise specified. Details may not equal totals due to rounding.

Month	Exports	Imports	Balance
January 2004	17.8	36.9	-19.1
February 2004	21.3	15.8	5.6
March 2004	19.3	30.7	-11.4
April 2004	30.7	15.9	14.8
May 2004	23.5	62.1	-38.6
June 2004	25.2	21.3	3.9
July 2004	25.6	37.2	-11.6
August 2004	28.3	79.2	-50.9
September 2004	53.4	22.9	30.5
October 2004	26.7	32.0	-5.4
November 2004	29.9	48.6	-18.7
December 2004	28.3	15.5	12.8
TOTAL 2004	330.1	418.0	-87.9

2005 : U.S. trade in goods with Oman

NOTE: All figures are in millions of U.S. dollars on a nominal basis, not seasonally adjusted unless otherwise specified. Details may not equal totals due to rounding.

Month	Exports	Imports	Balance
January 2005	14.5	47.5	-32.9
February 2005	26.4	112.3	-85.9
March 2005	84.6	14.2	70.5
April 2005	36.4	9.5	26.8
May 2005	38.7	44.3	-5.6
June 2005	39.5	54.0	-14.5
July 2005	43.2	55.7	-12.5
August 2005	32.5	16.9	15.6
September 2005	37.8	17.7	20.1
October 2005	55.8	71.7	-15.9
November 2005	111.0	16.1	94.9
December 2005	50.3	95.1	-44.8
TOTAL 2005	**570.7**	**555.0**	**15.7**

2001 : U.S. trade in goods with Morocco

NOTE: All figures are in millions of U.S. dollars on a nominal basis, not seasonally adjusted unless otherwise specified. Details may not equal totals due to rounding.

Month	Exports	Imports	Balance
January 2001	25.8	32.4	-6.6
February 2001	19.5	36.5	-17.0
March 2001	23.4	48.8	-25.4
April 2001	25.0	39.6	-14.6
May 2001	28.2	43.5	-15.3
June 2001	23.1	29.6	-6.5
July 2001	18.5	30.8	-12.3
August 2001	27.0	41.4	-14.4
September 2001	19.6	39.3	-19.7
October 2001	20.6	33.2	-12.6
November 2001	22.2	36.8	-14.6
December 2001	29.0	22.7	6.3
TOTAL 2001	281.9	434.6	-152.7

2002 : U.S. trade in goods with Morocco

NOTE: All figures are in millions of U.S. dollars on a nominal basis, not seasonally adjusted unless otherwise specified. Details may not equal totals due to rounding.

Month	Exports	Imports	Balance
January 2002	149.9	32.9	117.0
February 2002	142.1	24.2	117.9
March 2002	82.1	31.5	50.6
April 2002	18.3	28.3	-10.0
May 2002	16.7	28.7	-12.0
June 2002	24.6	30.6	-6.0
July 2002	20.7	46.2	-25.5
August 2002	19.5	33.4	-13.9
September 2002	16.0	29.4	-13.4
October 2002	30.3	34.1	-3.8
November 2002	20.6	38.0	-17.4
December 2002	24.7	35.1	-10.4
TOTAL 2002	565.5	392.4	173.1

2003 : U.S. trade in goods with Morocco

NOTE: All figures are in millions of U.S. dollars on a nominal basis, not seasonally adjusted unless otherwise specified. Details may not equal totals due to rounding.

Month	Exports	Imports	Balance
January 2003	74.7	37.1	37.6
February 2003	28.4	28.3	0.1
March 2003	25.7	26.5	-0.8
April 2003	33.1	29.4	3.8
May 2003	17.3	36.9	-19.7
June 2003	29.9	38.4	-8.6
July 2003	73.4	33.5	39.9
August 2003	39.3	33.5	5.8
September 2003	23.7	31.3	-7.6
October 2003	33.6	30.3	3.3
November 2003	40.6	28.6	12.0
December 2003	48.9	31.3	17.6
TOTAL 2003	468.5	385.2	83.3

2004 : U.S. trade in goods with Morocco

NOTE: All figures are in millions of U.S. dollars on a nominal basis, not seasonally adjusted unless otherwise specified. Details may not equal totals due to rounding.

Month	Exports	Imports	Balance
January 2004	84.2	45.2	39.1
February 2004	94.0	37.9	56.2
March 2004	27.0	49.6	-22.6
April 2004	21.5	33.6	-12.1
May 2004	47.3	34.5	12.8
June 2004	23.9	50.3	-26.4
July 2004	23.3	47.9	-24.6
August 2004	25.0	51.6	-26.6
September 2004	43.7	37.4	6.3
October 2004	31.3	50.8	-19.6
November 2004	33.1	38.3	-5.1
December 2004	43.9	38.2	5.7
TOTAL 2004	**498.3**	**515.2**	**-16.9**

2005 : U.S. trade in goods with Morocco

NOTE: All figures are in millions of U.S. dollars on a nominal basis, not seasonally adjusted unless otherwise specified. Details may not equal totals due to rounding.

Month	Exports	Imports	Balance
January 2005	50.2	39.8	10.4
February 2005	91.7	34.9	56.8
March 2005	71.7	28.3	43.4
April 2005	43.0	49.0	-5.9
May 2005	23.9	44.3	-20.4
June 2005	32.4	52.5	-20.1
July 2005	21.2	36.3	-15.1
August 2005	16.8	34.7	-18.0
September 2005	22.7	31.3	-8.7
October 2005	44.8	27.6	17.2
November 2005	34.0	28.5	5.5
December 2005	28.4	38.7	-10.3
TOTAL 2005	480.8	445.8	35.0

2007 : U.S. trade in goods with Morocco

NOTE: All figures are in millions of U.S. dollars on a nominal basis, not seasonally adjusted unless otherwise specified. Details may not equal totals due to rounding.

Month	Exports	Imports	Balance
January 2007	65.7	47.8	17.8
February 2007	130.5	42.8	87.8
March 2007	119.1	50.8	68.3
April 2007	91.4	49.6	41.8
May 2007	85.3	42.1	43.2
June 2007	67.6	48.1	19.5
July 2007	65.8	69.9	-4.0
August 2007	101.0	52.2	48.9
September 2007	141.6	47.9	93.7
October 2007	162.4	80.0	82.4
November 2007	151.2	37.4	113.8
December 2007	112.5	41.3	71.2
TOTAL 2007	1,294.2	609.9	684.2

2008 : U.S. trade in goods with Morocco

NOTE: All figures are in millions of U.S. dollars on a nominal basis, not seasonally adjusted unless otherwise specified. Details may not equal totals due to rounding.

Month	Exports	Imports	Balance
January 2008	121.4	54.5	66.9
February 2008	161.3	79.5	81.7
March 2008	192.4	98.6	93.8
April 2008	119.4	65.8	53.6
May 2008	55.7	62.2	-6.6
June 2008	150.2	69.5	80.7
July 2008	89.8	66.5	23.3
August 2008	147.5	104.3	43.2
September 2008	82.2	76.7	5.5
October 2008	94.0	69.1	24.9
November 2008	83.5	65.2	18.4
December 2008	138.4	66.8	71.6
TOTAL 2008	1,435.9	878.7	557.1

2009 : U.S. trade in goods with Morocco

NOTE: All figures are in millions of U.S. dollars on a nominal basis, not seasonally adjusted unless otherwise specified. Details may not equal totals due to rounding.

Month	Exports	Imports	Balance
January 2009	81.8	43.8	38.1
February 2009	114.7	31.9	82.7
March 2009	128.1	51.4	76.7
April 2009	172.4	42.4	129.9
May 2009	148.6	34.7	113.9
June 2009	86.9	35.9	51.0
July 2009	170.3	33.8	136.6
August 2009	138.7	44.8	93.9
September 2009	142.1	29.6	112.4
October 2009	129.6	39.7	89.9
November 2009	161.2	37.9	123.3
December 2009	155.9	42.0	113.9
TOTAL 2009	**1,630.3**	**468.0**	**1,162.3**

2010 : U.S. trade in goods with Morocco

NOTE: All figures are in millions of U.S. dollars on a nominal basis, not seasonally adjusted unless otherwise specified. Details may not equal totals due to rounding.

Month	Exports	Imports	Balance
January 2010	162.0	49.9	112.1
February 2010	197.7	46.8	150.9
March 2010	146.8	48.0	98.8
April 2010	202.5	60.2	142.3
May 2010	98.4	47.6	50.8
June 2010	150.1	56.7	93.5
July 2010	103.6	37.4	66.2
August 2010	150.0	43.3	106.7
September 2010	172.0	68.3	103.7
October 2010	256.8	59.8	197.0
November 2010	200.0	103.3	96.8
December 2010	106.9	64.0	42.9
TOTAL 2010	1,947.0	685.4	1,261.6

2011 : U.S. trade in goods with Morocco

NOTE: All figures are in millions of U.S. dollars on a nominal basis, not seasonally adjusted unless otherwise specified. Details may not equal totals due to rounding.

Month	Exports	Imports	Balance
January 2011	250.0	59.7	190.2
February 2011	175.7	133.9	41.8
March 2011	250.8	98.6	152.2
April 2011	187.8	55.4	132.4
May 2011	172.4	54.9	117.5
June 2011	255.0	138.6	116.4
July 2011	209.5	73.9	135.6
August 2011	250.9	68.1	182.8
September 2011	289.8	107.1	182.6
October 2011	181.2	64.2	117.0
November 2011	260.5	71.2	189.3
December 2011	338.9	70.0	268.9
TOTAL 2011	**2,822.4**	**995.6**	**1,826.8**

1996 : U.S. trade in goods with Jordan

NOTE: All figures are in millions of U.S. dollars on a nominal basis, not seasonally adjusted unless otherwise specified. Details may not equal totals due to rounding.

Month	Exports	Imports	Balance
January 1996	23.9	1.5	22.4
February 1996	24.9	1.5	23.4
March 1996	29.4	1.9	27.5
April 1996	32.1	1.9	30.2
May 1996	28.1	1.8	26.3
June 1996	30.4	3.3	27.1
July 1996	18.2	2.2	16.0
August 1996	45.4	2.6	42.8
September 1996	22.9	2.7	20.2
October 1996	34.3	2.1	32.2
November 1996	33.3	2.0	31.3
December 1996	22.3	1.7	20.6
TOTAL 1996	345.2	25.2	320.0

1997 : U.S. trade in goods with Jordan

NOTE: All figures are in millions of U.S. dollars on a nominal basis, not seasonally adjusted unless otherwise specified. Details may not equal totals due to rounding.

Month	Exports	Imports	Balance
January 1997	33.1	2.3	30.8
February 1997	29.0	1.3	27.7
March 1997	24.6	0.9	23.7
April 1997	28.2	2.3	25.9
May 1997	35.0	11.6	23.4
June 1997	38.4	0.5	37.9
July 1997	24.2	0.8	23.4
August 1997	27.6	0.8	26.8
September 1997	35.9	1.1	34.8
October 1997	48.3	1.0	47.3
November 1997	39.5	1.7	37.8
December 1997	38.7	1.0	37.7
TOTAL 1997	402.5	25.3	377.2

1998 : U.S. trade in goods with Jordan

NOTE: All figures are in millions of U.S. dollars on a nominal basis, not seasonally adjusted unless otherwise specified. Details may not equal totals due to rounding.

Month	Exports	Imports	Balance
January 1998	20.3	0.9	19.4
February 1998	21.0	0.5	20.5
March 1998	64.9	1.4	63.5
April 1998	35.9	1.0	34.9
May 1998	14.0	1.4	12.6
June 1998	47.2	1.4	45.8
July 1998	28.0	0.8	27.2
August 1998	23.0	1.4	21.6
September 1998	19.0	1.1	17.9
October 1998	30.2	2.9	27.3
November 1998	24.2	1.5	22.7
December 1998	25.3	2.1	23.2
TOTAL 1998	**353.0**	**16.4**	**336.6**

1999 : U.S. trade in goods with Jordan

NOTE: All figures are in millions of U.S. dollars on a nominal basis, not seasonally adjusted unless otherwise specified. Details may not equal totals due to rounding.

Month	Exports	Imports	Balance
January 1999	14.6	1.1	13.5
February 1999	20.4	1.8	18.6
March 1999	24.4	1.3	23.1
April 1999	27.7	0.7	27.0
May 1999	23.4	9.5	13.9
June 1999	19.2	2.5	16.7
July 1999	28.3	1.7	26.6
August 1999	37.6	3.4	34.2
September 1999	18.7	0.9	17.8
October 1999	20.8	3.3	17.5
November 1999	17.4	2.5	14.9
December 1999	23.2	2.0	21.2
TOTAL 1999	275.7	30.7	245.0

2000 : U.S. trade in goods with Jordan

NOTE: All figures are in millions of U.S. dollars on a nominal basis, not seasonally adjusted unless otherwise specified. Details may not equal totals due to rounding.

Month	Exports	Imports	Balance
January 2000	30.9	3.1	27.8
February 2000	17.4	3.1	14.3
March 2000	32.1	4.6	27.5
April 2000	25.1	3.1	22.0
May 2000	22.4	4.3	18.1
June 2000	22.6	5.9	16.7
July 2000	27.3	5.8	21.5
August 2000	34.7	7.0	27.7
September 2000	35.8	7.7	28.1
October 2000	24.0	9.1	14.9
November 2000	19.5	8.9	10.6
December 2000	25.1	10.7	14.4
TOTAL 2000	316.9	73.3	243.6

2002 : U.S. trade in goods with Jordan

NOTE: All figures are in millions of U.S. dollars on a nominal basis, not seasonally adjusted unless otherwise specified. Details may not equal totals due to rounding.

Month	Exports	Imports	Balance
January 2002	22.7	29.2	-6.5
February 2002	19.4	25.0	-5.6
March 2002	34.3	20.8	13.5
April 2002	28.8	24.6	4.2
May 2002	49.0	25.3	23.7
June 2002	25.4	21.0	4.4
July 2002	36.1	46.2	-10.1
August 2002	34.2	52.0	-17.8
September 2002	25.4	46.0	-20.6
October 2002	53.1	44.8	8.3
November 2002	48.8	35.5	13.3
December 2002	27.2	42.0	-14.8
TOTAL 2002	**404.4**	**412.4**	**-8.0**

2003 : U.S. trade in goods with Jordan

NOTE: All figures are in millions of U.S. dollars on a nominal basis, not seasonally adjusted unless otherwise specified. Details may not equal totals due to rounding.

Month	Exports	Imports	Balance
January 2003	35.1	44.0	-8.9
February 2003	20.7	40.9	-20.2
March 2003	91.1	48.6	42.5
April 2003	18.5	47.0	-28.5
May 2003	37.3	41.0	-3.6
June 2003	25.9	44.9	-19.1
July 2003	36.6	64.3	-27.7
August 2003	32.8	69.2	-36.4
September 2003	47.6	82.8	-35.2
October 2003	50.6	66.7	-16.1
November 2003	39.9	57.1	-17.2
December 2003	56.3	66.8	-10.5
TOTAL 2003	492.4	673.5	-181.0

2004 : U.S. trade in goods with Jordan

NOTE: All figures are in millions of U.S. dollars on a nominal basis, not seasonally adjusted unless otherwise specified. Details may not equal totals due to rounding.

Month	Exports	Imports	Balance
January 2004	46.5	71.0	-24.5
February 2004	39.2	74.0	-34.8
March 2004	40.4	84.6	-44.2
April 2004	41.4	64.1	-22.6
May 2004	41.9	68.6	-26.7
June 2004	56.0	83.9	-27.8
July 2004	37.6	91.5	-53.9
August 2004	37.3	76.1	-38.8
September 2004	34.6	141.8	-107.2
October 2004	57.0	119.7	-62.7
November 2004	63.1	118.8	-55.7
December 2004	56.5	99.3	-42.8
TOTAL 2004	**551.5**	**1,093.4**	**-541.9**

2005 : U.S. trade in goods with Jordan

NOTE: All figures are in millions of U.S. dollars on a nominal basis, not seasonally adjusted unless otherwise specified. Details may not equal totals due to rounding.

Month	Exports	Imports	Balance
January 2005	35.3	116.3	-81.0
February 2005	34.0	81.0	-47.0
March 2005	50.5	116.4	-65.9
April 2005	49.6	85.2	-35.6
May 2005	63.1	84.3	-21.2
June 2005	64.9	94.0	-29.0
July 2005	50.6	104.8	-54.2
August 2005	67.2	123.2	-56.0
September 2005	41.6	137.1	-95.6
October 2005	72.6	117.4	-44.9
November 2005	51.7	103.7	-52.0
December 2005	63.0	103.4	-40.4
TOTAL 2005	644.2	1,266.8	-622.7

2006 : U.S. trade in goods with Jordan

NOTE: All figures are in millions of U.S. dollars on a nominal basis, not seasonally adjusted unless otherwise specified. Details may not equal totals due to rounding.

Month	Exports	Imports	Balance
January 2006	55.2	100.9	-45.7
February 2006	43.1	103.5	-60.4
March 2006	62.9	121.4	-58.5
April 2006	45.9	108.7	-62.8
May 2006	50.4	111.4	-61.0
June 2006	57.4	103.8	-46.4
July 2006	68.3	138.0	-69.7
August 2006	60.6	133.3	-72.7
September 2006	45.7	144.7	-99.1
October 2006	51.3	126.5	-75.2
November 2006	45.5	113.1	-67.5
December 2006	64.1	116.8	-52.7
TOTAL 2006	**650.3**	**1,422.1**	**-771.7**

1999 : U.S. trade in goods with Australia

NOTE: All figures are in millions of U.S. dollars on a nominal basis, not seasonally adjusted unless otherwise specified. Details may not equal totals due to rounding.

Month	Exports	Imports	Balance
January 1999	828.9	396.9	432.0
February 1999	807.3	344.2	463.1
March 1999	921.5	345.2	576.3
April 1999	880.6	417.2	463.4
May 1999	929.3	466.9	462.4
June 1999	992.3	495.7	496.6
July 1999	900.1	442.2	457.9
August 1999	951.0	508.8	442.2
September 1999	1,143.0	495.4	647.6
October 1999	1,378.9	443.2	935.7
November 1999	1,094.3	445.2	649.1
December 1999	991.1	479.2	511.9
TOTAL 1999	11,818.3	5,280.1	6,538.2

2000 : U.S. trade in goods with Australia

NOTE: All figures are in millions of U.S. dollars on a nominal basis, not seasonally adjusted unless otherwise specified. Details may not equal totals due to rounding.

Month	Exports	Imports	Balance
January 2000	1,013.2	513.4	499.8
February 2000	998.2	381.2	617.0
March 2000	1,053.9	453.3	600.6
April 2000	1,116.5	526.5	590.0
May 2000	1,072.8	562.9	509.9
June 2000	1,136.5	588.3	548.2
July 2000	1,009.9	574.3	435.6
August 2000	1,086.2	587.2	499.0
September 2000	992.4	575.8	416.6
October 2000	1,011.9	514.3	497.6
November 2000	966.3	581.2	385.1
December 2000	1,024.6	579.6	445.0
TOTAL 2000	**12,482.4**	**6,438.0**	**6,044.4**

2001 : U.S. trade in goods with Australia

NOTE: All figures are in millions of U.S. dollars on a nominal basis, not seasonally adjusted unless otherwise specified. Details may not equal totals due to rounding.

Month	Exports	Imports	Balance
January 2001	856.5	542.0	314.5
February 2001	922.3	396.3	526.0
March 2001	990.3	522.6	467.7
April 2001	875.9	567.5	308.4
May 2001	881.8	554.1	327.7
June 2001	927.0	537.6	389.4
July 2001	890.2	581.7	308.5
August 2001	891.3	566.8	324.5
September 2001	883.7	597.1	286.6
October 2001	936.7	591.9	344.8
November 2001	879.1	542.2	336.9
December 2001	995.7	478.0	517.7
TOTAL 2001	**10,930.5**	**6,477.8**	**4,452.7**

2002 : U.S. trade in goods with Australia

NOTE: All figures are in millions of U.S. dollars on a nominal basis, not seasonally adjusted unless otherwise specified. Details may not equal totals due to rounding.

Month	Exports	Imports	Balance
January 2002	947.1	533.4	413.7
February 2002	917.0	397.4	519.6
March 2002	1,049.0	462.4	586.6
April 2002	954.6	580.6	374.0
May 2002	1,204.3	582.0	622.3
June 2002	1,140.6	513.9	626.7
July 2002	1,414.9	629.7	785.2
August 2002	1,027.5	570.8	456.7
September 2002	1,014.9	559.1	455.8
October 2002	1,139.2	565.8	573.4
November 2002	984.9	496.2	488.7
December 2002	1,290.9	587.5	703.4
TOTAL 2002	**13,084.9**	**6,478.8**	**6,606.1**

2003 : U.S. trade in goods with Australia

NOTE: All figures are in millions of U.S. dollars on a nominal basis, not seasonally adjusted unless otherwise specified. Details may not equal totals due to rounding.

Month	Exports	Imports	Balance
January 2003	836.7	567.7	269.0
February 2003	1,018.9	387.5	631.3
March 2003	992.3	470.5	521.8
April 2003	892.8	517.9	374.9
May 2003	1,047.7	593.1	454.6
June 2003	1,316.2	488.3	827.9
July 2003	1,388.5	564.3	824.2
August 2003	1,134.2	636.9	497.3
September 2003	1,156.7	500.7	656.0
October 2003	1,183.1	564.8	618.2
November 2003	1,030.1	551.4	478.8
December 2003	1,090.4	570.4	520.0
TOTAL 2003	13,087.6	6,413.7	6,673.9

2005 : U.S. trade in goods with Australia

NOTE: All figures are in millions of U.S. dollars on a nominal basis, not seasonally adjusted unless otherwise specified. Details may not equal totals due to rounding.

Month	Exports	Imports	Balance
January 2005	1,133.2	542.4	590.8
February 2005	1,170.7	417.0	753.7
March 2005	1,358.0	591.1	766.9
April 2005	1,313.2	595.7	717.4
May 2005	1,318.8	681.8	637.0
June 2005	1,339.7	658.0	681.7
July 2005	1,381.8	791.0	590.8
August 2005	1,315.7	608.3	707.5
September 2005	1,313.5	611.0	702.5
October 2005	1,265.6	607.9	657.7
November 2005	1,334.1	641.9	692.1
December 2005	1,344.2	596.0	748.3
TOTAL 2005	15,588.5	7,342.2	8,246.3

2006 : U.S. trade in goods with Australia

NOTE: All figures are in millions of U.S. dollars on a nominal basis, not seasonally adjusted unless otherwise specified. Details may not equal totals due to rounding.

Month	Exports	Imports	Balance
January 2006	1,464.8	657.2	807.7
February 2006	1,198.2	465.5	732.6
March 2006	1,437.6	719.6	717.9
April 2006	1,437.5	616.2	821.3
May 2006	1,416.3	677.4	738.9
June 2006	1,341.4	744.3	597.2
July 2006	1,452.1	799.0	653.1
August 2006	1,573.1	693.7	879.4
September 2006	1,500.0	646.8	853.2
October 2006	1,630.6	621.3	1,009.3
November 2006	1,552.0	787.9	764.2
December 2006	1,542.1	775.1	767.0
TOTAL 2006	17,545.7	8,204.0	9,341.7

2007 : U.S. trade in goods with Australia

NOTE: All figures are in millions of U.S. dollars on a nominal basis, not seasonally adjusted unless otherwise specified. Details may not equal totals due to rounding.

Month	Exports	Imports	Balance
January 2007	1,421.3	701.9	719.5
February 2007	1,409.2	510.9	898.3
March 2007	1,664.6	683.8	980.8
April 2007	1,414.3	690.1	724.2
May 2007	1,626.3	780.0	846.3
June 2007	1,596.2	725.5	870.7
July 2007	1,511.7	772.7	738.9
August 2007	1,737.6	862.7	874.9
September 2007	1,683.4	635.0	1,048.4
October 2007	1,719.9	782.9	937.0
November 2007	1,656.4	652.7	1,003.8
December 2007	1,737.3	816.9	920.4
TOTAL 2007	**19,178.2**	**8,615.0**	**10,563.2**

2008 : U.S. trade in goods with Australia

NOTE: All figures are in millions of U.S. dollars on a nominal basis, not seasonally adjusted unless otherwise specified. Details may not equal totals due to rounding.

Month	Exports	Imports	Balance
January 2008	1,518.9	907.2	611.8
February 2008	1,860.2	671.2	1,189.0
March 2008	2,111.6	624.7	1,487.0
April 2008	1,608.8	836.5	772.3
May 2008	2,014.0	906.0	1,108.0
June 2008	2,047.7	1,139.9	907.9
July 2008	2,092.9	1,024.0	1,068.9
August 2008	1,942.8	968.8	974.0
September 2008	1,835.6	1,068.4	767.2
October 2008	1,965.5	883.2	1,082.3
November 2008	1,758.6	772.7	985.9
December 2008	1,461.9	786.2	675.7
TOTAL 2008	22,218.6	10,588.8	11,629.8

┌─ 2009 : U.S. trade in goods with Australia ─

NOTE: All figures are in millions of U.S. dollars on a nominal basis, not seasonally adjusted unless otherwise specified. Details may not equal totals due to rounding.

Month	Exports	Imports	Balance
January 2009	1,357.5	782.6	574.9
February 2009	1,580.4	529.7	1,050.7
March 2009	1,833.2	682.9	1,150.2
April 2009	1,285.9	687.1	598.8
May 2009	1,528.2	582.3	945.9
June 2009	1,515.8	558.5	957.3
July 2009	1,393.8	660.0	733.7
August 2009	1,742.4	600.7	1,141.7
September 2009	1,631.7	702.0	929.7
October 2009	2,086.3	744.1	1,342.2
November 2009	1,735.0	729.5	1,005.5
December 2009	1,909.2	752.1	1,157.1
TOTAL 2009	**19,599.3**	**8,011.5**	**11,587.8**

1986 : U.S. trade in goods with Israel

NOTE: All figures are in millions of U.S. dollars on a nominal basis, not seasonally adjusted unless otherwise specified. Details may not equal totals due to rounding.

Month	Exports	Imports	Balance
January 1986	221.5	230.4	-8.9
February 1986	179.2	194.6	-15.4
March 1986	207.3	207.1	0.2
April 1986	185.9	172.7	13.2
May 1986	183.7	172.1	11.6
June 1986	144.2	203.4	-59.2
July 1986	196.5	221.0	-24.5
August 1986	200.3	178.3	22.0
September 1986	183.8	220.8	-37.0
October 1986	188.1	189.9	-1.8
November 1986	165.0	245.0	-80.0
December 1986	183.1	182.5	0.6
TOTAL 1986	2,238.6	2,417.8	-179.2

1987 : U.S. trade in goods with Israel

NOTE: All figures are in millions of U.S. dollars on a nominal basis, not seasonally adjusted unless otherwise specified. Details may not equal totals due to rounding.

Month	Exports	Imports	Balance
January 1987	135.0	194.3	-59.3
February 1987	158.2	215.5	-57.3
March 1987	263.5	240.7	22.8
April 1987	377.4	177.9	199.5
May 1987	227.3	194.2	33.1
June 1987	249.4	223.1	26.3
July 1987	291.8	270.1	21.7
August 1987	281.4	195.6	85.8
September 1987	296.3	233.7	62.6
October 1987	254.1	225.5	28.6
November 1987	313.9	219.3	94.6
December 1987	281.9	249.4	32.5
TOTAL 1987	**3,130.2**	**2,639.3**	**490.9**

1988 : U.S. trade in goods with Israel

NOTE: All figures are in millions of U.S. dollars on a nominal basis, not seasonally adjusted unless otherwise specified. Details may not equal totals due to rounding.

Month	Exports	Imports	Balance
January 1988	265.0	245.8	19.2
February 1988	186.9	235.0	-48.1
March 1988	276.2	247.2	29.0
April 1988	258.6	213.9	44.7
May 1988	313.9	256.3	57.6
June 1988	279.8	245.3	34.5
July 1988	316.9	271.0	45.9
August 1988	293.2	233.4	59.8
September 1988	254.5	224.4	30.1
October 1988	256.8	273.3	-16.5
November 1988	225.3	278.3	-53.0
December 1988	317.1	247.7	69.4
TOTAL 1988	3,244.2	2,971.6	272.6

1989 : U.S. trade in goods with Israel

NOTE: All figures are in millions of U.S. dollars on a nominal basis, not seasonally adjusted unless otherwise specified. Details may not equal totals due to rounding.

Month	Exports	Imports	Balance
January 1989	0.0	1.2	-1.2
February 1989	0.0	0.6	-0.6
March 1989	0.3	1.0	-0.7
April 1989	1.7	1.9	-0.2
May 1989	1.8	3.5	-1.7
June 1989	1.1	8.2	-7.1
July 1989	11.3	299.6	-288.3
August 1989	135.3	238.8	-103.5
September 1989	195.1	301.9	-106.8
October 1989	219.8	262.4	-42.6
November 1989	246.5	281.0	-34.5
December 1989	240.1	263.0	-22.9
TOTAL 1989	**1,053.0**	**1,663.1**	**-610.1**

1990 : U.S. trade in goods with Israel

NOTE: All figures are in millions of U.S. dollars on a nominal basis, not seasonally adjusted unless otherwise specified. Details may not equal totals due to rounding.

Month	Exports	Imports	Balance
January 1990	277.9	297.3	-19.4
February 1990	243.7	259.5	-15.8
March 1990	244.4	293.7	-49.3
April 1990	235.5	226.7	8.8
May 1990	238.8	255.4	-16.6
June 1990	229.5	260.3	-30.8
July 1990	261.8	322.8	-61.0
August 1990	267.3	244.8	22.5
September 1990	259.7	281.0	-21.3
October 1990	314.5	301.8	12.7
November 1990	327.6	301.2	26.4
December 1990	302.3	268.9	33.4
TOTAL 1990	3,203.0	3,313.4	-110.4

2001 : U.S. trade in goods with Bahrain

NOTE: All figures are in millions of U.S. dollars on a nominal basis, not seasonally adjusted unless otherwise specified. Details may not equal totals due to rounding.

Month	Exports	Imports	Balance
January 2001	28.2	40.0	-11.8
February 2001	24.3	48.0	-23.7
March 2001	56.8	34.4	22.4
April 2001	20.3	25.5	-5.2
May 2001	23.3	24.9	-1.6
June 2001	22.9	38.7	-15.8
July 2001	40.7	31.1	9.6
August 2001	70.0	26.0	44.0
September 2001	34.7	28.0	6.7
October 2001	28.9	27.7	1.2
November 2001	28.0	41.1	-13.1
December 2001	54.7	58.6	-3.9
TOTAL 2001	432.8	424.0	8.8

2002 : U.S. trade in goods with Bahrain

NOTE: All figures are in millions of U.S. dollars on a nominal basis, not seasonally adjusted unless otherwise specified. Details may not equal totals due to rounding.

Month	Exports	Imports	Balance
January 2002	21.3	43.8	-22.5
February 2002	21.9	32.2	-10.3
March 2002	26.1	26.6	-0.5
April 2002	35.7	28.1	7.6
May 2002	45.1	25.7	19.4
June 2002	37.5	25.6	11.9
July 2002	42.5	27.0	15.5
August 2002	58.3	33.9	24.4
September 2002	26.0	34.6	-8.6
October 2002	52.6	31.1	21.5
November 2002	27.0	41.0	-14.0
December 2002	25.5	45.1	-19.6
TOTAL 2002	419.5	394.7	24.8

2003 : U.S. trade in goods with Bahrain

NOTE: All figures are in millions of U.S. dollars on a nominal basis, not seasonally adjusted unless otherwise specified. Details may not equal totals due to rounding.

Month	Exports	Imports	Balance
January 2003	24.6	49.0	-24.4
February 2003	227.2	59.1	168.1
March 2003	34.0	60.8	-26.7
April 2003	32.0	43.0	-11.0
May 2003	24.4	15.4	9.0
June 2003	25.7	20.1	5.6
July 2003	21.1	30.3	-9.2
August 2003	20.2	14.5	5.7
September 2003	23.0	19.3	3.7
October 2003	24.3	17.6	6.7
November 2003	28.9	24.0	4.9
December 2003	23.0	25.2	-2.2
TOTAL 2003	508.4	378.2	130.2

2004 : U.S. trade in goods with Bahrain

NOTE: All figures are in millions of U.S. dollars on a nominal basis, not seasonally adjusted unless otherwise specified. Details may not equal totals due to rounding.

Month	Exports	Imports	Balance
January 2004	19.1	31.7	-12.6
February 2004	19.8	25.4	-5.6
March 2004	33.7	32.4	1.3
April 2004	25.0	24.3	0.6
May 2004	21.8	36.5	-14.7
June 2004	25.9	25.5	0.4
July 2004	25.1	21.5	3.6
August 2004	24.5	46.7	-22.2
September 2004	21.7	32.8	-11.1
October 2004	28.3	57.4	-29.1
November 2004	27.4	42.1	-14.7
December 2004	29.5	28.9	0.6
TOTAL 2004	301.8	405.3	-103.5

2005 : U.S. trade in goods with Bahrain

NOTE: All figures are in millions of U.S. dollars on a nominal basis, not seasonally adjusted unless otherwise specified. Details may not equal totals due to rounding.

Month	Exports	Imports	Balance
January 2005	24.2	47.8	-23.6
February 2005	27.3	31.5	-4.3
March 2005	29.1	33.7	-4.6
April 2005	36.2	20.5	15.7
May 2005	29.7	26.0	3.7
June 2005	27.3	21.8	5.5
July 2005	20.1	29.7	-9.6
August 2005	35.6	39.6	-4.0
September 2005	33.7	44.3	-10.6
October 2005	29.3	60.6	-31.3
November 2005	27.3	39.7	-12.5
December 2005	31.0	36.3	-5.3
TOTAL 2005	**350.8**	**431.6**	**-80.8**

2007 : U.S. trade in goods with Bahrain

NOTE: All figures are in millions of U.S. dollars on a nominal basis, not seasonally adjusted unless otherwise specified. Details may not equal totals due to rounding.

Month	Exports	Imports	Balance
January 2007	44.2	45.6	-1.4
February 2007	43.2	60.2	-17.0
March 2007	57.2	72.6	-15.4
April 2007	46.2	79.1	-32.9
May 2007	39.9	82.5	-42.5
June 2007	44.6	33.8	10.8
July 2007	36.9	33.9	3.0
August 2007	38.0	64.8	-26.7
September 2007	48.1	58.1	-10.0
October 2007	67.5	25.1	42.4
November 2007	67.0	27.1	39.9
December 2007	58.4	41.7	16.6
TOTAL 2007	591.3	624.6	-33.2

2008 : U.S. trade in goods with Bahrain

NOTE: All figures are in millions of U.S. dollars on a nominal basis, not seasonally adjusted unless otherwise specified. Details may not equal totals due to rounding.

Month	Exports	Imports	Balance
January 2008	37.4	26.1	11.3
February 2008	44.0	65.6	-21.6
March 2008	64.5	28.5	36.0
April 2008	129.7	46.0	83.7
May 2008	61.3	37.1	24.3
June 2008	55.9	31.4	24.5
July 2008	48.5	50.0	-1.5
August 2008	50.2	58.6	-8.4
September 2008	57.1	40.1	17.0
October 2008	62.7	91.3	-28.7
November 2008	108.8	39.2	69.5
December 2008	109.5	25.1	84.4
TOTAL 2008	829.5	538.9	290.6

2009 : U.S. trade in goods with Bahrain

NOTE: All figures are in millions of U.S. dollars on a nominal basis, not seasonally adjusted unless otherwise specified. Details may not equal totals due to rounding.

Month	Exports	Imports	Balance
January 2009	58.1	48.7	9.4
February 2009	48.8	28.6	20.3
March 2009	57.3	37.7	19.6
April 2009	50.5	38.6	11.9
May 2009	40.3	54.1	-13.8
June 2009	81.8	22.1	59.7
July 2009	58.2	24.7	33.4
August 2009	36.1	38.1	-1.9
September 2009	72.8	44.4	28.4
October 2009	51.7	47.9	3.9
November 2009	64.1	36.6	27.4
December 2009	47.6	41.9	5.6
TOTAL 2009	667.4	463.5	203.9

2010 : U.S. trade in goods with Bahrain

NOTE: All figures are in millions of U.S. dollars on a nominal basis, not seasonally adjusted unless otherwise specified. Details may not equal totals due to rounding.

Month	Exports	Imports	Balance
January 2010	132.0	39.2	92.8
February 2010	37.2	51.7	-14.6
March 2010	59.7	31.4	28.3
April 2010	45.0	39.0	6.0
May 2010	69.0	20.2	48.8
June 2010	144.4	25.8	118.6
July 2010	222.0	31.0	191.0
August 2010	55.8	32.8	23.0
September 2010	63.9	25.3	38.6
October 2010	271.8	35.2	236.6
November 2010	74.6	29.8	44.8
December 2010	74.2	58.7	15.5
TOTAL 2010	**1,249.6**	**420.3**	**829.3**

2011 : U.S. trade in goods with Bahrain

NOTE: All figures are in millions of U.S. dollars on a nominal basis, not seasonally adjusted unless otherwise specified. Details may not equal totals due to rounding.

Month	Exports	Imports	Balance
January 2011	84.8	29.7	55.1
February 2011	236.4	55.2	181.2
March 2011	79.2	52.0	27.2
April 2011	94.6	33.6	61.1
May 2011	75.8	33.5	42.3
June 2011	68.1	33.8	34.2
July 2011	62.2	46.0	16.2
August 2011	109.1	71.2	37.9
September 2011	74.8	32.1	42.7
October 2011	97.9	35.7	62.2
November 2011	113.3	50.7	62.6
December 2011	116.7	44.9	71.8
TOTAL 2011	**1,213.0**	**518.4**	**694.6**

2006 : U.S. trade in goods with Colombia

NOTE: All figures are in millions of U.S. dollars on a nominal basis, not seasonally adjusted unless otherwise specified. Details may not equal totals due to rounding.

Month	Exports	Imports	Balance
January 2006	460.6	778.2	-317.7
February 2006	461.6	710.3	-248.7
March 2006	549.7	809.4	-259.6
April 2006	492.0	796.4	-304.4
May 2006	561.6	889.6	-328.0
June 2006	557.9	846.1	-288.2
July 2006	510.4	959.0	-448.6
August 2006	589.5	743.8	-154.3
September 2006	609.5	817.1	-207.6
October 2006	631.6	758.2	-126.7
November 2006	622.4	596.4	26.1
December 2006	661.9	561.2	100.7
TOTAL 2006	**6,708.6**	**9,265.7**	**-2,557.1**

2007 : U.S. trade in goods with Colombia

NOTE: All figures are in millions of U.S. dollars on a nominal basis, not seasonally adjusted unless otherwise specified. Details may not equal totals due to rounding.

Month	Exports	Imports	Balance
January 2007	603.2	736.3	-133.1
February 2007	621.6	652.0	-30.4
March 2007	689.2	642.6	46.6
April 2007	603.0	594.8	8.2
May 2007	652.0	706.4	-54.4
June 2007	703.4	732.0	-28.6
July 2007	696.8	924.5	-227.7
August 2007	807.9	939.2	-131.3
September 2007	756.0	830.6	-74.5
October 2007	809.0	855.3	-46.3
November 2007	809.3	865.0	-55.6
December 2007	806.1	954.9	-148.8
TOTAL 2007	8,557.7	9,433.6	-875.9

2008 : U.S. trade in goods with Colombia

NOTE: All figures are in millions of U.S. dollars on a nominal basis, not seasonally adjusted unless otherwise specified. Details may not equal totals due to rounding.

Month	Exports	Imports	Balance
January 2008	855.4	1,065.5	-210.1
February 2008	947.6	989.3	-41.7
March 2008	1,082.6	912.5	170.2
April 2008	973.2	1,170.9	-197.8
May 2008	905.5	1,345.7	-440.3
June 2008	906.7	1,096.1	-189.5
July 2008	1,058.2	1,334.1	-275.9
August 2008	1,187.0	1,421.4	-234.4
September 2008	932.8	1,074.7	-141.9
October 2008	1,000.9	1,029.8	-29.0
November 2008	784.5	854.9	-70.4
December 2008	803.0	798.3	4.7
TOTAL 2008	**11,437.3**	**13,093.2**	**-1,655.9**

2009 : U.S. trade in goods with Colombia

NOTE: All figures are in millions of U.S. dollars on a nominal basis, not seasonally adjusted unless otherwise specified. Details may not equal totals due to rounding.

Month	Exports	Imports	Balance
January 2009	709.1	690.1	18.9
February 2009	739.1	698.6	40.5
March 2009	820.9	793.5	27.4
April 2009	663.7	966.1	-302.4
May 2009	675.4	795.4	-120.1
June 2009	715.1	1,013.1	-298.1
July 2009	752.6	1,077.6	-325.0
August 2009	755.6	1,011.1	-255.5
September 2009	841.0	1,102.9	-261.9
October 2009	958.3	1,061.3	-103.1
November 2009	858.4	943.0	-84.6
December 2009	962.5	1,170.3	-207.9
TOTAL 2009	9,451.5	11,323.1	-1,871.7

2010 : U.S. trade in goods with Colombia

NOTE: All figures are in millions of U.S. dollars on a nominal basis, not seasonally adjusted unless otherwise specified. Details may not equal totals due to rounding.

Month	Exports	Imports	Balance
January 2010	896.2	1,061.3	-165.1
February 2010	1,019.5	1,172.0	-152.6
March 2010	1,129.2	1,101.7	27.5
April 2010	1,049.8	1,397.3	-347.4
May 2010	906.8	1,195.6	-288.8
June 2010	847.4	1,367.3	-519.9
July 2010	1,022.5	1,412.4	-389.9
August 2010	983.1	1,379.5	-396.3
September 2010	930.9	1,264.0	-333.0
October 2010	1,109.3	1,262.9	-153.6
November 2010	1,028.5	1,631.4	-602.9
December 2010	1,146.2	1,414.0	-267.8
TOTAL 2010	**12,069.3**	**15,659.3**	**-3,590.0**

2012 : U.S. trade in goods with Colombia

NOTE: All figures are in millions of U.S. dollars on a nominal basis, not seasonally adjusted unless otherwise specified. Details may not equal totals due to rounding.

Month	Exports	Imports	Balance
January 2012	1,159.1	2,023.5	-864.4
February 2012	1,108.5	2,048.8	-940.3
March 2012	1,428.2	2,333.7	-905.5
April 2012	1,315.2	2,163.0	-847.8
May 2012	1,361.0	2,348.7	-987.7
June 2012	1,273.0	1,933.2	-660.2
July 2012	1,200.1	1,798.5	-598.4
August 2012	1,441.7	2,118.7	-677.0
September 2012	1,688.1	2,069.8	-381.7
October 2012	1,380.5	1,980.4	-599.8
November 2012	1,474.4	1,945.2	-470.8
December 2012	1,564.8	1,868.9	-304.1
TOTAL 2012	**16,394.6**	**24,632.4**	**-8,237.8**

2002 : U.S. trade in goods with Peru

NOTE: All figures are in millions of U.S. dollars on a nominal basis, not seasonally adjusted unless otherwise specified. Details may not equal totals due to rounding.

Month	Exports	Imports	Balance
January 2002	124.6	157.3	-32.7
February 2002	121.7	128.6	-6.9
March 2002	126.9	136.6	-9.7
April 2002	135.2	132.6	2.6
May 2002	156.8	147.7	9.1
June 2002	127.4	132.7	-5.3
July 2002	131.6	163.6	-32.0
August 2002	119.4	170.1	-50.7
September 2002	112.8	173.1	-60.3
October 2002	126.4	207.2	-80.8
November 2002	153.0	198.2	-45.2
December 2002	126.7	191.6	-64.9
TOTAL 2002	1,562.5	1,939.3	-376.8

2003 : U.S. trade in goods with Peru

NOTE: All figures are in millions of U.S. dollars on a nominal basis, not seasonally adjusted unless otherwise specified. Details may not equal totals due to rounding.

Month	Exports	Imports	Balance
January 2003	127.6	175.0	-47.4
February 2003	143.0	178.2	-35.2
March 2003	168.2	195.3	-27.2
April 2003	133.1	169.3	-36.2
May 2003	128.0	157.1	-29.1
June 2003	134.4	179.3	-44.9
July 2003	155.3	191.0	-35.8
August 2003	166.5	217.8	-51.3
September 2003	130.4	154.9	-24.5
October 2003	124.0	255.0	-131.0
November 2003	154.4	269.9	-115.5
December 2003	133.6	265.7	-132.1
TOTAL 2003	**1,698.5**	**2,408.7**	**-710.2**

2004 : U.S. trade in goods with Peru

NOTE: All figures are in millions of U.S. dollars on a nominal basis, not seasonally adjusted unless otherwise specified. Details may not equal totals due to rounding.

Month	Exports	Imports	Balance
January 2004	145.1	228.8	-83.8
February 2004	155.7	262.1	-106.3
March 2004	180.4	245.7	-65.3
April 2004	142.3	247.8	-105.5
May 2004	196.5	212.0	-15.5
June 2004	143.8	248.4	-104.6
July 2004	186.6	304.2	-117.6
August 2004	179.2	343.2	-164.0
September 2004	175.3	368.1	-192.8
October 2004	190.1	403.2	-213.1
November 2004	211.1	405.9	-194.8
December 2004	194.8	432.2	-237.4
TOTAL 2004	**2,101.0**	**3,701.6**	**-1,600.5**

2005 : U.S. trade in goods with Peru

NOTE: All figures are in millions of U.S. dollars on a nominal basis, not seasonally adjusted unless otherwise specified. Details may not equal totals due to rounding.

Month	Exports	Imports	Balance
January 2005	212.6	331.8	-119.2
February 2005	169.6	396.8	-227.2
March 2005	174.3	396.4	-222.0
April 2005	199.4	343.2	-143.8
May 2005	222.2	418.8	-196.7
June 2005	213.7	375.5	-161.9
July 2005	183.8	407.4	-223.6
August 2005	207.2	475.2	-268.0
September 2005	165.1	497.1	-332.0
October 2005	178.7	427.6	-248.9
November 2005	179.6	547.9	-368.3
December 2005	203.3	501.4	-298.1
TOTAL 2005	2,309.4	5,119.2	-2,809.7

2006 : U.S. trade in goods with Peru

NOTE: All figures are in millions of U.S. dollars on a nominal basis, not seasonally adjusted unless otherwise specified. Details may not equal totals due to rounding.

Month	Exports	Imports	Balance
January 2006	234.4	481.1	-246.7
February 2006	223.5	457.3	-233.8
March 2006	238.3	530.2	-291.9
April 2006	243.2	376.6	-133.4
May 2006	192.0	538.1	-346.1
June 2006	268.1	496.9	-228.7
July 2006	189.4	455.1	-265.8
August 2006	240.2	529.5	-289.4
September 2006	220.4	544.0	-323.6
October 2006	290.3	487.3	-197.1
November 2006	314.6	503.6	-189.0
December 2006	272.5	480.6	-208.1
TOTAL 2006	**2,926.8**	**5,880.4**	**-2,953.5**

2008 : U.S. trade in goods with Peru

NOTE: All figures are in millions of U.S. dollars on a nominal basis, not seasonally adjusted unless otherwise specified. Details may not equal totals due to rounding.

Month	Exports	Imports	Balance
January 2008	453.2	472.7	-19.5
February 2008	361.7	525.1	-163.4
March 2008	570.2	423.3	146.9
April 2008	468.7	503.6	-34.9
May 2008	519.3	440.2	79.1
June 2008	626.5	548.4	78.1
July 2008	584.5	658.8	-74.3
August 2008	763.0	423.5	339.5
September 2008	508.5	524.2	-15.8
October 2008	526.2	540.8	-14.7
November 2008	384.3	412.4	-28.1
December 2008	416.7	339.3	77.4
TOTAL 2008	6,183.0	5,812.5	370.5

2009 : U.S. trade in goods with Peru

NOTE: All figures are in millions of U.S. dollars on a nominal basis, not seasonally adjusted unless otherwise specified. Details may not equal totals due to rounding.

Month	Exports	Imports	Balance
January 2009	372.1	405.0	-32.9
February 2009	318.0	254.1	64.0
March 2009	369.6	331.6	38.0
April 2009	334.7	331.6	3.0
May 2009	381.1	291.6	89.6
June 2009	410.5	346.9	63.6
July 2009	429.4	358.3	71.1
August 2009	503.3	354.1	149.2
September 2009	460.2	407.7	52.5
October 2009	462.1	341.1	121.0
November 2009	422.3	327.0	95.3
December 2009	455.5	474.3	-18.8
TOTAL 2009	**4,918.8**	**4,223.3**	**695.5**

┌─ 2010 : U.S. trade in goods with Peru ─────────

NOTE: All figures are in millions of U.S. dollars on a nominal basis, not seasonally adjusted unless otherwise specified. Details may not equal totals due to rounding.

Month	Exports	Imports	Balance
January 2010	511.7	380.0	131.7
February 2010	511.5	390.4	121.2
March 2010	511.5	405.5	106.1
April 2010	600.7	419.4	181.3
May 2010	506.1	246.1	260.0
June 2010	485.7	390.4	95.3
July 2010	596.1	460.2	135.9
August 2010	552.5	481.6	70.8
September 2010	598.3	488.0	110.3
October 2010	623.0	445.3	177.7
November 2010	648.3	417.9	230.5
December 2010	608.7	532.2	76.5
TOTAL 2010	6,754.3	5,056.9	1,697.3

2011 : U.S. trade in goods with Peru

NOTE: All figures are in millions of U.S. dollars on a nominal basis, not seasonally adjusted unless otherwise specified. Details may not equal totals due to rounding.

Month	Exports	Imports	Balance
January 2011	661.7	681.9	-20.2
February 2011	616.8	456.2	160.5
March 2011	631.2	513.5	117.7
April 2011	709.5	490.7	218.9
May 2011	804.4	367.2	437.3
June 2011	685.5	592.1	93.4
July 2011	683.4	455.7	227.7
August 2011	719.3	689.7	29.6
September 2011	573.7	639.2	-65.5
October 2011	755.7	528.8	227.0
November 2011	789.4	569.2	220.2
December 2011	704.8	620.7	84.1
TOTAL 2011	**8,335.5**	**6,604.7**	**1,730.8**

2012 : U.S. trade in goods with Peru

NOTE: All figures are in millions of U.S. dollars on a nominal basis, not seasonally adjusted unless otherwise specified. Details may not equal totals due to rounding.

Month	Exports	Imports	Balance
January 2012	700.4	593.5	106.9
February 2012	663.6	548.9	114.7
March 2012	864.1	430.3	433.8
April 2012	786.5	409.1	377.4
May 2012	729.1	482.9	246.2
June 2012	701.2	488.9	212.3
July 2012	835.1	591.2	243.8
August 2012	869.8	531.2	338.6
September 2012	743.4	550.2	193.2
October 2012	814.6	555.6	259.0
November 2012	769.5	692.1	77.4
December 2012	880.1	552.6	327.5
TOTAL 2012	**9,357.3**	**6,426.5**	**2,930.8**

1999 : U.S. trade in goods with Chile

NOTE: All figures are in millions of U.S. dollars on a nominal basis, not seasonally adjusted unless otherwise specified. Details may not equal totals due to rounding.

Month	Exports	Imports	Balance
January 1999	262.2	282.0	-19.8
February 1999	248.7	259.3	-10.6
March 1999	236.2	304.4	-68.2
April 1999	228.0	265.3	-37.3
May 1999	234.4	193.2	41.2
June 1999	263.5	215.5	48.0
July 1999	227.9	207.9	20.0
August 1999	258.5	204.7	53.8
September 1999	226.3	236.6	-10.3
October 1999	260.6	293.7	-33.1
November 1999	266.2	246.8	19.4
December 1999	365.8	243.9	121.9
TOTAL 1999	3,078.3	2,953.3	125.0

2000 : U.S. trade in goods with Chile

NOTE: All figures are in millions of U.S. dollars on a nominal basis, not seasonally adjusted unless otherwise specified. Details may not equal totals due to rounding.

Month	Exports	Imports	Balance
January 2000	249.5	319.2	-69.7
February 2000	231.0	300.5	-69.5
March 2000	304.8	349.5	-44.7
April 2000	274.1	292.0	-17.9
May 2000	280.9	217.6	63.3
June 2000	243.5	216.5	27.0
July 2000	250.6	228.9	21.7
August 2000	405.0	230.8	174.2
September 2000	308.6	229.6	79.0
October 2000	306.2	263.8	42.4
November 2000	329.4	289.4	40.0
December 2000	276.9	331.2	-54.3
TOTAL 2000	3,460.5	3,269.0	191.5

2001 : U.S. trade in goods with Chile

NOTE: All figures are in millions of U.S. dollars on a nominal basis, not seasonally adjusted unless otherwise specified. Details may not equal totals due to rounding.

Month	Exports	Imports	Balance
January 2001	249.9	390.5	-140.6
February 2001	258.5	291.4	-32.9
March 2001	270.2	386.1	-115.9
April 2001	239.1	365.8	-126.7
May 2001	264.4	271.3	-6.9
June 2001	256.3	225.4	30.9
July 2001	393.6	269.3	124.3
August 2001	252.9	236.8	16.1
September 2001	235.4	256.9	-21.5
October 2001	251.8	218.0	33.8
November 2001	227.4	253.2	-25.8
December 2001	218.8	330.5	-111.7
TOTAL 2001	**3,118.3**	**3,495.2**	**-376.9**

2002 : U.S. trade in goods with Chile

NOTE: All figures are in millions of U.S. dollars on a nominal basis, not seasonally adjusted unless otherwise specified. Details may not equal totals due to rounding.

Month	Exports	Imports	Balance
January 2002	219.9	447.4	-227.5
February 2002	209.6	350.6	-141.0
March 2002	226.5	361.6	-135.1
April 2002	212.7	414.2	-201.5
May 2002	217.0	276.0	-59.0
June 2002	240.5	269.9	-29.4
July 2002	192.7	233.9	-41.2
August 2002	215.8	289.4	-73.6
September 2002	211.6	246.9	-35.3
October 2002	207.6	266.6	-59.0
November 2002	222.2	252.8	-30.6
December 2002	232.7	375.2	-142.5
TOTAL 2002	2,608.8	3,784.5	-1,175.7

2003 : U.S. trade in goods with Chile

NOTE: All figures are in millions of U.S. dollars on a nominal basis, not seasonally adjusted unless otherwise specified. Details may not equal totals due to rounding.

Month	Exports	Imports	Balance
January 2003	195.7	400.2	-204.6
February 2003	192.8	319.3	-126.5
March 2003	231.2	389.7	-158.4
April 2003	233.3	401.6	-168.3
May 2003	202.3	276.4	-74.1
June 2003	227.0	252.4	-25.4
July 2003	255.4	262.3	-6.9
August 2003	233.3	253.1	-19.8
September 2003	213.7	260.8	-47.1
October 2003	255.4	245.8	9.5
November 2003	215.5	252.5	-37.0
December 2003	259.5	391.3	-131.8
TOTAL 2003	**2,715.0**	**3,705.4**	**-990.4**

2005 : U.S. trade in goods with Chile

NOTE: All figures are in millions of U.S. dollars on a nominal basis, not seasonally adjusted unless otherwise specified. Details may not equal totals due to rounding.

Month	Exports	Imports	Balance
January 2005	315.9	670.3	-354.4
February 2005	365.9	544.7	-178.8
March 2005	446.2	521.1	-74.9
April 2005	525.4	622.8	-97.4
May 2005	473.2	539.4	-66.2
June 2005	440.5	344.1	96.4
July 2005	525.3	456.0	69.3
August 2005	386.8	520.2	-133.3
September 2005	380.2	489.3	-109.1
October 2005	383.4	536.9	-153.5
November 2005	506.0	625.0	-119.0
December 2005	384.7	794.6	-409.9
TOTAL 2005	5,133.5	6,664.3	-1,530.8

2006 : U.S. trade in goods with Chile

NOTE: All figures are in millions of U.S. dollars on a nominal basis, not seasonally adjusted unless otherwise specified. Details may not equal totals due to rounding.

Month	Exports	Imports	Balance
January 2006	477.9	843.3	-365.4
February 2006	365.2	739.3	-374.1
March 2006	557.7	858.1	-300.5
April 2006	501.2	749.9	-248.7
May 2006	561.1	760.3	-199.2
June 2006	656.8	855.1	-198.3
July 2006	596.7	760.9	-164.1
August 2006	486.9	912.2	-425.2
September 2006	473.3	936.7	-463.4
October 2006	534.7	792.2	-257.5
November 2006	902.2	545.7	356.5
December 2006	472.1	811.5	-339.3
TOTAL 2006	6,585.8	9,565.1	-2,979.3

2007 : U.S. trade in goods with Chile

NOTE: All figures are in millions of U.S. dollars on a nominal basis, not seasonally adjusted unless otherwise specified. Details may not equal totals due to rounding.

Month	Exports	Imports	Balance
January 2007	493.0	941.0	-448.0
February 2007	553.6	770.7	-217.1
March 2007	649.4	818.9	-169.5
April 2007	604.4	832.7	-228.2
May 2007	720.8	800.0	-79.3
June 2007	724.8	554.4	170.3
July 2007	680.4	817.0	-136.6
August 2007	734.4	854.5	-120.1
September 2007	658.0	643.7	14.3
October 2007	728.9	701.6	27.3
November 2007	749.3	522.8	226.5
December 2007	851.1	741.4	109.8
TOTAL 2007	**8,148.1**	**8,998.8**	**-850.7**

2008 : U.S. trade in goods with Chile

NOTE: All figures are in millions of U.S. dollars on a nominal basis, not seasonally adjusted unless otherwise specified. Details may not equal totals due to rounding.

Month	Exports	Imports	Balance
January 2008	741.6	766.6	-25.0
February 2008	940.1	868.2	71.9
March 2008	993.8	776.1	217.7
April 2008	1,075.1	815.4	259.7
May 2008	1,277.6	713.8	563.8
June 2008	1,337.3	521.1	816.3
July 2008	1,221.3	795.8	425.5
August 2008	1,039.1	763.5	275.6
September 2008	806.9	605.0	201.9
October 2008	957.1	500.6	456.5
November 2008	814.1	468.4	345.7
December 2008	653.3	601.4	51.9
TOTAL 2008	11,857.4	8,196.0	3,661.5

2009 : U.S. trade in goods with Chile

NOTE: All figures are in millions of U.S. dollars on a nominal basis, not seasonally adjusted unless otherwise specified. Details may not equal totals due to rounding.

Month	Exports	Imports	Balance
January 2009	747.9	731.5	16.4
February 2009	575.1	601.9	-26.8
March 2009	637.9	716.7	-78.8
April 2009	811.8	508.0	303.9
May 2009	829.9	419.7	410.2
June 2009	716.3	346.2	370.2
July 2009	784.6	459.9	324.7
August 2009	713.2	340.9	372.3
September 2009	696.4	431.8	264.6
October 2009	732.2	395.8	336.4
November 2009	1,066.7	423.3	643.4
December 2009	1,033.5	573.6	460.0
TOTAL 2009	9,345.6	5,949.3	3,396.4

BIBLIOGRAPHY

Baker, Fred W. US to Strengthen Defense Relationship with Chile. Last modified 2012.http:// www.defense.gov/News/NewsArticle.aspx?ID=47689.

Behar, Alberto. The Impact of North-South and South-South Trade Agreements on Bilateral Trade. Last modified September 2010. http://www.freit.org/WorkingPapers/Papers/ TradePolicyRegional/FREIT220.pdf.

Blank, Rebecca M. Kappos, David, J. March 2012. Intellectual Property and the US Economy: Industries in Focus. http://www.uspto.gov/news/publications/IP_Report_March_2012.pdf.

Berrigan, Frida, and Wingo, Jonathan. The Bush Effect: US Military Involvement in Latin America Rises, Development and Humanitarian Aid Fall. Last modified November 5, 2005. http://www.commondreams.org/views05/1105-21.htm.

Bussey, Jane. US Military: Mission: Possible. Last modified December 1, 2010. http://latintrade. com/2010/12/u-s-military-mission-possible.

Canto, Victor A. US Trade Policy: History and Evidence. Last modified 2011.http://www.cato. org/doc-download/sites/cato.org/files/serials/files/cato-journal/2011/10/cj3n3-4.pdf.

Celaya, Fernando. Bolivia-Peru Relationship Increasingly Similar to That Between Colombia-Venezuela. Last modified August 27, 2009. http://spanishsecurityworld.wordpress. com/2009/08/27/bolivia-peru-relationship-increasingly-similar-to-that-between-colombia-venezuela/.

Chanlett-Avery, Emma. Thailand: Background and US Relations. Last modified June 5, 2012. http://www.fas.org/sgp/crs/row/RL32593.pdf.

Chile Free Trade Agreement. Last modified 2013. http://www.ustr.gov/trade-agreements/ free-trade-agreements/chile-fta/final-text.

Committee on Foreign Relations United States Senate. Treaties and Other International Agreements: The Role of the United States Senate. Last modified January 2001.http://www.gpo. gov/fdsys/pkg/CPRT-106SPRT66922/pdf/CPRT-106SPRT66922.pdf.

Cooper, William H. Free Trade Agreements: Impact on US Trade and Implications for US Trade Policy. Last modified June 18, 2012.http://www.fas.org/sgp/crs/row/RL31356.pdf.

Cooper, William H. Trade Agreements: Impact on US Trade and Implications for US Trade Policy. Last modified July 10, 2007. http://fpc.state.gov/documents/organization/89919.pdf.

Cronin, Audrey Kurth. Foreign Terrorist Organizations. Last modified February 6, 2004. http://www.fas.org/irp/crs/RL32223.pdf.

Dangl, Benjamin. US Bases in Colombia Rattle the Region. Last modified March 2010. http://progressive.org/danglmarch10.html.

De Gregorio, Jose. The Chilean Economy in the Current Global Financial Crisis. Last modified November 2008.http://www.bcentral.cl/politicas/presentaciones/consejeros/pdf/2008/jdg18112008.pdf.

Dull, Jonathan R.A. Diplomatic History of the American Revolution. Last modified 1985. http://www.loc.gov/rr/program/bib/ourdocs/alliance.html.

Dufour, Jules. The Worldwide Network of US Military Bases: The Global Deployment of US Military Personnel. Last modified February 17, 2013.http://www.globalresearch.ca/the-worldwide-network-of-us-military-bases/5564.

Espinel, Victoria. April 11, 2012. Intellectual Property and the US Economy.http://www.whitehouse.gov/blog/2012/04/11/intellectual-property-and-us-economy.

Forham, Benjamin O. Protectionist Empire: Trade, Tariffs, and United States Foreign Policy, 1890-1914. Last modified 2011. http://government.arts.cornell.edu/assets/psac/sp11/Fordham_PSAC_Mar11.pdf.

Fossey, Ellie. Understanding and Evaluating Qualitative Research. Last modified 2002 http://www.utas.edu.au/__data/assets/pdf_file/0018/165204/fossey-et-al-evaluating-qual-research.pdf.

Free Trade Agreement Reports. Office of the United States Representative. Last modified 2013. http://www.ustr.gov/archive/Trade_Agreements/Bilateral/Chile_FTA/Reports/Section_Index.html.

Free Trade with Peru. Last modified June 2007. http://www.ustr.gov/sites/default/files/uploads/factsheets/2007/asset_upload_file585_13067.pdf.

Gazette, Phuket. Looking Back: A Brief History of Thai-US Relations. Last modified July 4, 2012.http://www.phuketgazette.net/phuketlifestyle/savepdf.php?ref=20127531133&id=16337.

Golinger, Eva. Washington behind the Honduras coup: Here is the evidence. Last modified July 15, 2009. http://www.globalresearch.ca/washington-behind-the-honduras-coup-here-is-the-evidence/14390

Gowen, Brian. April 25, 2012. The Importance of Intellectual Property in the US.http://americaandtheglobaleconomy.wordpress.com/2012/04/25/the-importance-of-intellectual-property-in-the-u-s/.

Grimmett, Jeanne J. Dispute Settlement under the U.S.-Peru Trade Promotion Agreement: An Overview. Last modified August 12, 2011. http://www.nationalaglawcenter.org/assets/crs/RS22752.pdf.

Gusterson, Hugh. *People of the Bomb: Portraits of America's Nuclear Complex*. University of Minnesota Press. 2004.

Hagan, Kevin. Taking Advantage of Free Trade Agreements in Order to Export. Last modified January 30, 2008. http://voices.yahoo.com/taking-advantage-free-trade-agreements-order-845137.html.

Hartmut, Hillgenberg. A Fresh Look at Soft Law. Last modified 1999. http://www.ejil.org/pdfs/10/3/597.pdf.

Healey, Declan. The US-Colombia Free Trade Agreement—A Historical Placement of the FTA. Last modified August 2010. http://via.library.depaul.edu/cgi/viewcontent.cgi?article=1053&context=etd.

Hornbeck, J.E. US-Latin American Trade: Recent Trends and Policy Issues. Last modified February 8, 2011.http://www.fas.org/sgp/crs/row/98-840.pdf.

International Trade. Advisory Committee System Should Be Updated to Better Serve US Policy Needs. Last modified September 2002. http://www.gao.gov/new.items/d02876.pdf.

Irwin, Douglas. From Smoot-Hawley to Reciprocal Trade Agreement: Changing the Course of US Trade Policy in the 1930s. Last modified January 1998. http://www.nber.org/chapters/c6899.pdf.

Israel, Jonathan. *The Dutch Republic: Its Rise, Greatness, and Fall 1477-1806*. Oxford History of Early Modern Europe. 1995.

Kartaraz. Peru and Bolivian Relations Deteriorate. Last modified June 17, 2009.http://www.zimbio.com/Bolivia/articles/712G3E2_jA-/Peru+Bolivian+relations+deteriorate.

Katzman, Kenneth. Bahrain: Reform, Security, and US Policy. Last modified February 12, 2013. http://www.fas.org/sgp/crs/mideast/95-1013.pdf.

Kirgis, Frederic. International Agreements and U.S. Law. Last modified May 1997. http://www.asil.org/insigh10.cfm.

Klein, Aaron. How a US Radar Station in the Negev Affect a Potential Israel-Iran Clash. Last modified May 30, 2012.http://www.time.com/time/world/article/0,8599,2115955,00.html.

Koplan, Stephen. US-Bahrain Free Trade Agreement: Potential Economy wide and Selected Sectoral Effects. Last modified October 2004. http://www.usitc.gov/publications/332/pub3726.pdf.

Kurnamaev, Anatoly. US Will Keep Importing Oil from Colombia, Venezuela, IEA Says. Last modified February 7, 2013.http://www.bloomberg.com/news/2013-02-07/u-s-will-keep-importing-oil-from-colombia-venezuela-iea-says.html.

Lindsey, John. Pentagon Building Bases in Central America and Colombia. Last modified January 27, 2011.http://forusa.org/blogs/john-linsay-poland/pentagon-building-bases-central-america-colombia/8445.

Long, Andrew. Trading for Security: Military Alliances and Economic Agreements. Last modified 2001.http://atop.rice.edu/download/publications/LongLeedsJPR.pdf.

McCausland, Jeffery, and Stuart, Douglas. US-UK Relations at the Start of the 21st Century. Last modified January 2006.http://www.strategicstudiesinstitute.army.mil/pdffiles/pub633.pdf.

Meyer, Nico. Bilateral and Regional Trade Agreements and Technical Barriers to Trade: An African Perspective. Johannesburg. 2010.

Miller, Terry. Defining Economic Freedom. Last modified 2011.http://thf_media.s3.amazonaws.com/index/pdf/2011/Index2011_Chapter2.pdf.

Moore, Michael. Relationship between US and Swedish Militaries.US-Sweden Defense Industry Conference. Last modified June 10, 2009.http://www.ndia.org/Divisions/Divisions/International/Documents/Michael%20Moore%20-%20Relationship%20between%20U.S.%20and%20Swedish%20militaries.pdf.

Moran, Lee. The Marine Corps Heads Down Under: US to set up base in Australia to ward off growing China threat. Last modified November 14, 2011. http://www.dailymail.co.uk/news/article-2060412/U-S-Marines-set-base-Australia-bid-beat-threat-China—sparking-fears-terror-target.html.

Morrison, Wayne.China-US Trade Issues. Last modified May 21, 2012. http://www.fas.org/sgp/crs/row/RL33536.pdf.

NAFTA has had its trade-offs for the U.S.—Los Angeles Times. 2008. Last modified March 5, 2013. http://articles.latimes.com/2008/mar/03/business/fi-nafta3.

Norden, Deborah. The Rise of the Lieutenant Colonels. Last modified November 29, 2012. http://pdfs.postprefix.com/venezuela/2634108.pdf.

Pallares, Jose Hidalgo. Argentina, in Venezuela's Footsteps. Last modified July 2, 2012. http://www.atfa.org/argentina-in-venezuelas-footsteps/.

Peacock, Kasey. Cobra Gold Begins in Thailand. Last modified February 8, 2012. http://www. army.mil/article/73324/.

Pearson, Daniel. US-Korea Free Trade Agreement: Potential Economy-Wide and Selected Sectoral Effects. Last modified 2007. http://www.usitc.gov/publications/332/pub3949.pdf.

Pierre-Marie Dupuy. Soft law and the International Law of The Environment. Last modified 1991.http://data.sfb.bg.ac.rs/sftp/foper2/Dupuy%20%20Scft%20Law%20and%20the%20 international%20law%20of%20the%20environment.pdf.

Pizarro, Rodrigo. The Free Trade Agreement between the USA and Chile: An Instrument of US Commercial Interest. Last modified February 2006. http://www.networkideas.org/working/ oct2006/02_2006.pdf.

Plummer, Michael G., Cheong, David, and Hamanaka, Shintaro. Methodology for Impact Assessment of Free Trade Agreements. http://www.iadb.org/intal/intalcdi/PE/2011/07645.pdf.

Robertson, John K. A Brief Profile of the Continental Army. Last modified 2008. http:// revwar75.com/ob/intro.htm.

Rowden, William H. Port of Haifa Study: Summary Report. Last modified May 1993.http:// www.cna.org/sites/default/files/research/2793008910.pdf.

Salazar, Jose M. The US-Central America Free Trade Agreement: Opportunities and Challenges. Last modified 1997.http://www.iie.com/publications/chapters_preview/375/09iie3616.pdf.

Schott, Jeffrey J. Assessing US FTA Policy. Last modified November 2004.http://www. petersoninstitute.org/publications/chapters_preview/375/13iie3616.pdf.

Schoultz, Lars. *Beneath the United States: A History of US Policy toward Latin America*. Cambridge: (Harvard University Press). 1998.

Teare, Richard W. US Marines to Darwin, Australia: Evolution of an Idea. Last modified November 18, 2011.http://cogitasia.com/u-s-marines-to-darwin-australia-evolution-of-an-idea/.

The Executive Branch | The White House. Last modified March 5, 2013.http://www.whitehouse. gov/our-government/executive-branch.

Topoleski, John J. Trade Adjustment Assistant for Workers (TAA) and Reemployment Trade Adjustment Assistance (RTAA).Last modified September 24, 2010. http://www.aging.senate.gov/ crs/aging6.pdf.

Trade Agreements. Last modified 2012. http://www.ustr.gov/trade-agreements.

Trade Agreements. Office of the United States Trade Representative. Last modified 2013. http:// www.ustr.gov/trade-agreements.

Treaty Affairs Staff. Treaties in Force: A List of Treassties and Other International Agreements of the United States in Force on January 1, 2012. Last modified 2012. http://www.state.gov/documents/organization/202293.pdf.

US-Chile Free Trade Agreement: Potential Economy wide and Selected Sectoral Effects. June 2003. http://www.usitc.gov/publications/332/pub3605.pdf

US-Colombia Trade Promotion Agreement Implementation Instructions. Tuesday, May 15, 2012. http://www.cbp.gov/xp/cgov/trade/trade_programs/international_agreements/free_trade/cotpa/cotpa_instructions.xml.

Vick, Carl, and Klein, Aaron J. How a US Radar Station in the Negev Affects a Potential Israel-Iran Clash. Last modified 2012.http://www.time.com/time/world/article/0,8599,2115955,00.html.

Vine, David. How US Taxpayers Are Paying the Pentagon to Occupy the Planet. Last modified December 14, 2012.http://www.aljazeera.com/indepth/opinion/2012/12/20121213122226666895.html.

Walser, Ray. US-Colombia Free Trade Agreement: Will the U.S. Miss a Historic Opportunity? Last modified October 6, 2011.http://www.heritage.org/research/reports/2011/10/us-colombia-free-trade-agreement-will-the-us-miss-a-historic-opportunity.

Zanotti, Jim. Israel: Background and U.S. Relations. Last modified November 7, 2012. http://www.fas.org/sgp/crs/mideast/RL33476.pdf.

Zoellick, Robert. Free Trade Agreement: Case of US-Australia Free Trade Agreement (AUSFTA). Last modified May 2004. http://faculty.arts.ubc.ca/nmalhotra/Misc/AUSFTA-HOM-Model.pdf.